# MISSING

# BANNERS

Matt,

I hope you enjoy
the topic.

Go Hoosiers!

## Tom Brew & Terry Hutchens

**ISBN Number:** 978-0-9858021-4-3

**Hilltop30 Publishers, LLC**
P.O. Box 973
Schererville, Indiana 46375

**E-mail**: tombrewsports@gmail.com

**Website:** www.Hilltop30.com

*For my favorite starting five,*
*my three children and my two granddaughters.*

*And for my brothers and my Mom,*
*who's still the biggest IU fan I know.*

*–Tom Brew*

*To my four cornerstones:*
*Dena, Susan, Bryan and Kevin.*

*–Terry Hutchens*

*For all the Indiana players and coaches*
*who were so generous of their time*
*to help make this project a success.*

*And lastly, for the great and loyal*
*IU fan base, which makes all this worth doing.*

*–Tom Brew & Terry Hutchens*

# _Missing Banners_

# Chapter 1

Stroll into Assembly Hall at Indiana University and you can't help but immediately glance up at that south wall. They hang as a testament to the greatness of this legendary basketball program, those five national championship banners.

They are us, and we are them. For every player that slips on an IU jersey, it's all about putting in thousands of hours of work – of giving up blood, sweat and tears in pursuit of another national title. And for every fan that walks into that iconic arena, it's all about that pride thing, too. It's those banners that remind us of Indiana's greatness through the years. For a devoted Hoosier fan, it's an honor to see those banners rocking ever so slightly in the breeze on game nights when the Hall is packed to the gills with 17,000-plus adoring fans.

It doesn't matter if you've just walked into the arena on game day or if you're the first one to walk into a cold gym in the morning for practice. The lights in the arena don't even have to be on. They are there, on the wall, and you know it.

It's as if the banners are there tapping you on the shoulder and saying, 'Hey, look at me. Look at what is truly important when it comes to Indiana basketball.' "

Legendary coaches Branch McCracken and Bob Knight were a big part of adding banners. So were many great players, like Marvin Huffman, Don Schlundt and Bobby "Slick" Leonard, like Quinn Buckner and Scott May, like Isiah Thomas and Steve Alford.

On those teams that won, once the banner goes up it's like

When Assembly Hall first opened in the early 1970s, there were only two lonely banners hanging in the south end zone. Quinn Buckner (21) and his teammates would start to work on changing that.

a symbol of approval, that all the hard work was worth it. The banners mean that much.

They are a symbol of success, a 10-foot by 20-foot stamp of approval. A symbol of a job well done.

"Once they put that banner up, they can't ever take it away from you," said Scott May, the national player of the year who led the unbeaten Hoosiers to the 1976 title. "After we won, it's like who really cares about what happened those other years? We got the job done."

May's classmate, point guard Quinn Buckner, concurs. He was there in 1973 when IU lost in the Final Four, and he was there in 1975 when Indiana was undefeated and on their way to a national title when May broke his arm and everything changed. After 31 wins in a row, IU lost to Kentucky 92-90 in the regional finals, and a season ended in heart-ripping pain.

Indiana went undefeated the next year and hung a banner, which took plenty of the pain away from the '75 ending. But not for everyone. For those seniors in 1975, great IU players like Steve Green and John Laskowski, not having a banner of their own still hurts, even 40 years later.

"There isn't a time when I've walked into Assembly Hall – and I've been there, what, probably a thousand times – where I don't look up there and think something's missing," said Laskowski, who's been around the program for almost all of those 40-plus years since he arrived in Bloomington from South Bend and a baby-faced teenager. "And trust me, I look up there at that wall every single time I walk into that building."

Ah, the missing banners. For all the joy the national championship years have brought to the Hoosier Nation, it's the close calls – the near-misses – that are so close to our hearts as well.

Five banners are nice, and we're proud of those. But there

3

should be more. Many, many more.

The banners mean that much, to everyone who walks into Assembly Hall. And the pursuit for more it what drives so many people.

*** *** ***

**J**ordan Hulls definitely had that kind of banner-hanging experience when he was being recruited by Indiana. Hulls was an Indiana boy who grew up in Bloomington, just down the road from

**Mike Dickbernd/IU Athletics**

When Jordan Hulls (left) got a late-night call from IU coach Tom Crean during his senior year in high school, he knew it was time to live a dream and commit to Indiana. They would rebuild this proud program together.

the IU campus, and played basketball at Bloomington South.

He will never forget the night Tom Crean called back in 2008. It was around 10 p.m. and the IU coach asked Hulls if he could meet him at Assembly Hall.

The backdrop of the story was that Hulls was scheduled to take a recruiting trip to Purdue the next day. Crean had heard about it and wasn't about to have Hulls' first in-state offer come from the arch-rivals to the north in West Lafayette.

So Crean called Hulls and invited him to come down to Assembly Hall. Jordan hopped in his father's truck and the two of them drove over to the arena.

"When we walked in, there was a scene right out of a movie in front of us," Hulls recalled when he wrote the foreword for the book "*Hoosiers Through and Through,*" written in 2014 by Terry Hutchens. "As we walked in the arena, there was nothing but spotlights on the banners and dim lights on the court, just enough to make the spotlights really stand out.

"We gathered and talked down at center court on the state of Indiana logo, and we just admired the banners."

That was all it took. Soon thereafter, Hulls committed to Indiana and the rest is history.

Ah, the magic of the banners. They mean a lot to a lot of people

Matt Roth wasn't an Indiana kid and didn't have any emotional connection to the banners before he committed to IU. But he remembers that all changing – and quickly – on his recruiting visit.

"When I got recruited coming out of high school and walking into Assembly Hall that first time, that's the first thing you see," said Roth, who grew up in Washington, Ill. "I don't even remember what the coaches were talking to me about when we walked into the door. But when you walk on that court, they're right there and they're in your face. It was one of the reasons – if not the biggest reason – why I chose Indiana. As a player, you always know that with Indiana people there is always the expectation of winning a national championship."

Dane Fife knows exactly what Roth is talking about. He grew up in Michigan but his earliest memories of the recruiting process at Indiana involve walking into Assembly Hall and being in the presence of those banners. And like Roth, Fife said those banners carry with them a sense of expectation.

"There's a lot of pride in earning a banner at Indiana and with that comes a great deal of pressure, too," said Fife, a member of the 2002 IU basketball team that is remembered as the only Indiana basketball team to play for a national championship and not close the deal.

"National championships are part of the expectation at Indiana," Fife said. "It doesn't matter now that it hasn't happened since 1987. That just makes people that much hungrier. Every year you open the season with that goal in mind and every year that you don't achieve it, it's just a little bit disappointing."

Fife said that every time a legendary Indiana basketball figure would come back and talk with his team when he was a player at IU from 1999-2002, he would be reminded not only of the expectations that those banners provided but something more – a responsibility to those who came before you.

"When Scott May walks into the building or Quinn Buckner or Isiah Thomas, you feel a sense of pride at the things that they were able to accomplish at Indiana," Fife said. "But you also get the feeling of responsibility to them to put up that sixth national championship banner."

Roth said there wasn't a practice he participated in at Indiana where he didn't at least once gaze up at the banners.

"When you're in a tough conditioning drill or a tough practice, that's all the incentive you need, to look up there and know that in our case there are five teams that expect a great deal out of the players who are there," Roth said. "I think there are a lot of teams that probably felt cheated that they didn't get that title, but at the same time it's all about the opportunity."

***    ***    ***

**Indiana basketball is all** about tradition. Whether it's the candy-striped warm-up pants, no names on the back of the jerseys or the fact that no numbers have ever been retired in the program, there is a feeling of reverence for IU basketball within those close to the program.

The national championship banners, and the other banners on the north end of the arena, just add to that tradition.

It also adds to that feeling you get when you walk into the arena each and every time.

"The mystique is still there," said Indianapolis radio personality Greg Rakestraw. "You've got a wall reserved only for national titles. That says a lot.

"Look at the Big Ten ad this year that shows the coast-to-coast spread of the league. What pops up to represent IU? Five banners. That tells you what you need to know."

Don Fischer, the radio play-by-play voice of Indiana basketball, said for 29 years and counting that one end of Assembly Hall has never changed. He said the north end changes from time to time with things that "are not nearly as important."

"But the banners are what Indiana basketball is all about," Fischer said. "To me, there is absolutely no question that the banners are the single biggest factor in the IU basketball tradition."

7

Bob Knight and his Hoosiers stand along the sidelines at Assembly Hall during the national anthem prior to a game in late 1974. They were looking up at the flag, of course, not the banners.

Scott Dolson, IU's deputy athletics director, was a student manager for the 1987 IU national championship team. And while he admits it has been nearly 30 years since Indiana has raised a new national championship banner, he said they still represent a tradition like no other.

"Some people try to say that it doesn't matter as much to the kids today because they weren't born when Indiana last had a national champion, but I don't agree," Dolson said. "I remember the first time I looked up at those banners and I wondered about the 1940 team and then the '53 team, too. Those teams always will hold a special place in IU history, just like the ones that came later. I think every year when March Madness comes around, the kids of today realize just how special those five banners hanging in Assembly Hall continue to be."

Jeremy Gray, IU's associate athletic director for strategic communications and fan experience, believes there is strong evidence that the banners mean as much as ever.

"I help oversee our social media efforts here at IU Athletics," Gray said. "About half the Facebook and Twitter profile pictures of IU fans that I see are of themselves standing in front of the banners. The banners are everywhere. Their mystique is as strong as ever."

How they came about is historic, too.

\*\*\*  \*\*\*  \*\*\*

The banners first came into being when the new Assembly Hall opened its doors in December of 1971. That coincided with the arrival of Indiana basketball coach Bob Knight that season.

The banners were Knight's idea to initially honor those IU

9

teams that had excelled on the national stage.

Thanks, Coach.

Chuck Crabb, the longtime public address announcer at Assembly Hall and IU's assistant athletic director for facilities, was in his final two years of undergraduate study at IU and working in Athletic Publicity as a student aide when Assembly Hall opened.

Crabb said it was Knight who made the banner idea happen.

"Coach talked about having banners saluting championships won in national competition, because a Big Ten championship was expected each year for Indiana University basketball," Crabb said. "That's why the many conference titles during his 29 years were not celebrated with individual banners.

"It was the national titles that mattered to him."

Crabb said Knight likely worked through athletic director Bill Orwig's lead lieutenant, assistant athletic director Bob Dro, to create the big banners honoring the 1940 and 1953 national championship teams. First evidence of those two banners hanging in Assembly Hall can be found in a 1973 game photograph.

No one can remember the existence of any banners commemorating IU's first two national champions before the current Assembly Hall opened its doors in 1971. Longtime Bloomington Herald-Times Sports Editor Bob Hammel said there may have been some sort of display in the lobby of the Seventh Street Fieldhouse that housed IU basketball from 1928-60. But he never remembered any banners.

Kit Klingelhoffer, a former associate athletic director, said unequivocally that banners did not exist in the "New Fieldhouse" that was the predecessor to Assembly Hall. That building hosted Indiana basketball from 1960-71 and is now known as the Gladstein Fieldhouse. It was resurfaced and holds indoor events for the

IU track and field teams.

After Knight had the two national champion banners erected in Assembly Hall, he and his players then went to work to add more. They did, in 1976, 1981 and 1987. And for nearly three decades, those five banners have hung proudly in Assembly Hall, waiting for some more company.

Many IU teams have come close, so so close. The pursuit of the sixth banner – and a seventh and eighth, and so on – never stops. Nor should it at this proud basketball school.

There are other banners that fly in Assembly Hall, but for years they have been on the north wall of Assembly Hall, across the court from the five national championship banners. Knight had a banner raised for IU's Final Four appearance in 1973, then the CCA banner in 1974 and the 1975 undefeated regular season and UPI national championship banner that saluted the '75 team.

Knight did make one exception regarding his feelings toward Big Ten individual season banners on Senior Night in 1983, when, according to Crabb, he announced just before the seniors spoke that a banner that would be known as the "People's Banner" would recognize the great fan support that helped the Hoosiers to a Big Ten title.

"Indiana needed to win its final three games – all at home – against conference contenders Purdue, Illinois and Ohio State," Crabb said. "Coach spoke about needing fan support, and it came in the form of some of the loudest crowds during Assembly Hall's 40-plus years."

The banner policy changed after Knight left the school in September 2000. In 2001, Big Ten championship banners were created on the north end for both the men and the women's teams, listing each year the program won a conference title. In addition, a banner honoring Final Four participation was put up.

Tom Crean applied the same philosophy that Knight did in '83 when he announced in 2013 that a banner would be raised for that team's outright Big Ten title, honoring the players who helped rebuild IU basketball after former coach Kelvin Sampson had nearly destroyed the program.

Former IU player Derek Elston, who was part of that resurgence under Crean, said when you walk into Assembly Hall, your eyes look in one of two directions – either at the national title banners or the other banners in the north end of the arena.

He said the 2013 banner, for obvious reasons, is the first place he looks. It is among the banners in the north end of the arena.

"What our group of guys had to endure over a four-year span – and for some, a three-year span – is something that not a lot of college athletes will ever have to go through," Elston said. "So

IU Archinves P-0055970

Much of the credit for creating the championship banners goes to Bob Knight. He instigated the plan to install them in the new Assembly Hall.

when I look over and see that 2013 Big Ten Championship banner, I picture a group of guys that fought and battled for not just each other but for the fans who were there in the stands cheering us on every game when they had nothing to cheer for."

The 2013 individual banner didn't go over well with everyone, though. One former player, Jarrad Odle, who played on the 2002 national runner-up team, didn't feel it was necessary and shared his feelings with Crean.

"We had a conversation that didn't go particularly well because I didn't agree with the whole idea of putting up a separate banner for the 2013 team," Odle said. "Not because they didn't deserve their Big Ten championship, but I just didn't feel like they were any different or any more special than all of the other Big Ten championships that we had earned, or the tradition.

"So for me I think that shows you right there how passionate I am about the banners actually hanging up and who represents what those banners actually mean."

*** *** ***

**According to Crabb, the banners** originally came from Annin Flagmakers Company in Verona, N.J., the nation's largest flag manufacturing company. In later years, Flag and Banner Company in Indianapolis took over as IU's banner provider.

"They maintained the same type font line as Annin and were local, permitting us to be involved in every step of the process," Crabb said.

Crabb said the last complete set of five NCAA banners came in 1987. Flag and Banner remade the north end basic banners in 2001, remade the 1983 banner in 2010, the 2013 banner before the 2013-2014 season and the AIAW Final Four Banner in 2014.

The banners are lowered before each spring commencement ceremony in Assembly Hall, which permits IATSE Local 618 stage-hand members to use a lint/fabric brush like you'd use on your good suits or dress pants to brush off the top and bottom sleeved areas and check on the condition of each banner. According to Crabb, they attract dust but don't really get dirty hanging over the court.

Still, they are carefully cared for. As well they should. They mean that much to every member of Hoosier Nation, players and fans alike.

*** *** ***

**So many former players** talked about what the banners meant to them in the recruiting process.

Jared Jeffries, like Hulls several years later, was an Indiana Mr. Basketball from Bloomington. But he said the belief that he could be part of a banner-hanging team was why he ultimately chose the Hoosiers over Duke.

"Coach Knight made me believe that I had a chance to hang a banner up there," Jeffries said. " Coach told me that he had never coached a player like me at Indiana and that always meant a lot because there had been a lot of great players come through there. That's one of the most disappointing things about never getting the chance to play for him. But there's no doubt that thinking that I had a chance to hang another banner there and believing what coach Knight said had a big role in my decision to go to Indiana."

Tom Coverdale, who played on the 2002 team that reached the national final, grew up a huge IU fan with a dream to wear the

14

cream and crimson. The first time he heard from Indiana, he told them that if they offered a scholarship he would take it because that was where he wanted to be and where his heart was.

"I had been to games there and just thought it was the best place in the world out of all the places I had been because that's what I had grown up watching," Coverdale said. "So then in the summer before my senior year when they offered I just remember Coach Knight saying, 'Take a couple of days and talk to your family,' and I didn't need those days. I just said, 'No, Coach. It's done. I'm coming.' "

Coverdale said the banners contributed to the whole experience.

"For me it was a big thing because I wanted to go there and the banners meant a lot to me," Coverdale said. "I think it meant something to guys like Dane (Fife) and Newt (Jeff Newton) and guys who weren't from Indiana. That's what made us so good. Everybody from Indiana, when you go there, the banners mean so much. But when you have out-of-state guys that it means that much to as well, that's what made us good."

Yogi Ferrell, who was a freshman starter on the No. 1-ranked 2013 team, said his reason for attending IU was all about the banners.

"As an Indiana kid, going to an Indiana school and hanging a banner possibly, I mean that's going to be remembered for the rest of your life," Ferrell said. "People are going to remember you as being on the 2000-such team that hung a banner. That was definitely the motivation for me to come here. It was close to home and that played into the decision, too, but the thought of what that banner would mean to people in the future was the driving force behind me attending IU."

*** *** ***

**W**hile the banners definitely represent the best of times for Indiana basketball, they can also be a reminder to those who didn't realize that dream of just how close they had come. For some former players, it has been hard to gaze upon them in the years after they left IU.

Christian Watford has been back to Assembly Hall on a few occasions and he said when he looks at those championship banners, it's like a punch in the gut.

"That was supposed to have been our year (2013) and we positioned ourselves where we needed to be and then we didn't

IU Archives P-0022376

For Indiana's Dane Fife (center, with hand in air), the idea of raising another banner in Assembly Hall meant everything to him. Advancing to the Final Four in 2002 got him very close to accomplishing that goal.

16

finish the job," Watford said. "When I look up there, the first thing I think is that no one on our team was even born the last time that Indiana won a national championship. And we thought we were going to be the ones that changed that. That's the hardest part, just knowing that we were close but couldn't get it done."

Watford said he would like to look back and think that all the hard work put in to set themselves up for a title run had been worth it.

Looking back, he's not sure he can say that. A missing banner can be that painful.

"It's just hard when we think about how we let that one get away from us," Watford said. "We put in so much time and people dedicated so much to it, and it just makes it tough to deal with."

Tom Coverdale said it's difficult to walk into Assembly Hall today and look up at those banners without getting an odd feeling.

"When you walk back in there and you see the five banners hanging and there isn't that sixth one up there, it's hard," Coverdale said. "You definitely feel like there should be a sixth one up there, as close as we got against Maryland."

It doesn't take much for Odle to think about 'What If?' when it comes to being reminded that his 2002 team came as close to any team in IU history to hanging a national championship banner without actually doing so.

The 2002 team remains the only team in IU history to get to the national championship game and not close the deal.

Odle said he remembered watching an interview recently from Assembly Hall where a television reporter was interviewing IU's Yogi Ferrell. As is often the case in canned interviews from inside the arena, the five national championship banners could be seen in the background of the interview.

17

For Odle, that's all it took. He said he was walking past his television at home, saw the interview, saw the banners, and got a sick feeling in his stomach.

"I always think to myself, 'How can you get that close and not do it?' " Odle said. "The reality is that there's a team every single year that gets that close and doesn't do it. But it just seems different when you play basketball at Indiana because those banners become such a part of the fabric of your life and a daily reminder of what you aspire to do."

Odle's 2002 teammate, Kyle Hornsby, has those same 'What If?' thoughts. He was in Assembly Hall early in the 2014-15 season when former IU coach Mike Davis brought his Texas Southern team to town to play the Hoosiers. He said looking at the banners that night was bittersweet.

"I would have loved to have had a career where I exited high school and I didn't have to look back and say 'What if?' and I would have loved to have had a college career where I didn't have to look back and say 'What if?' " Hornsby said. "While I'm proud to have that Big Ten championship mention on a banner up there – and I'm proud to have the national runner-up with that banner up there – its's still a 'What if?'

"I would have enjoyed it if we had been able to hang that sixth banner, but at the same time I'm still proud of what we were able to accomplish."

Elston said while it's easy for him to gaze upon the 2013 Big Ten title banner, it's not as simple to look at the five banners hanging at the other end of the arena.

That, he said, is a little too painful.

"I hate thinking about what would have, could have, or should have happened," Elston said. "To sit back and say we didn't have a national championship team is ridiculous to say. We had a group of guys that were more focused on bringing Bloomington a championship than literally anything else. The thing about reaching the tournament is once you're there, you don't have to be the best team, you just have to be the best team on that night. And Syracuse just played better than us that night."

***    ***    ***

**T**hen there's this, wondering if you'll ever see those banners again.

That was the feeling Dan Dakich had back in February 2008. Dakich had grown up in Northwest Indiana and remembered as a kid watching IU raise banners in 1976 and 1981. He was part of several great IU teams and is best known for shutting down Michael Jordan in an IU upset of North Carolina in 1984. He was also an assistant coach for years under Knight and returned to Bloomington during the Sampson era after a successful career coaching at Bowling Green.

Sampson, who had cheated like crazy at Oklahoma, had been caught doing the same thing at Indiana. Things were on the verge of exploding after word of thousands of impermissible phone calls to recruits came to light.

Dakich, then director of basketball operations, had nothing to do with Sampson's actions but when he got a call late one night from then-athletic director Rick Greenspan, he figured it was over.

He thought he'd never step foot in Assembly Hall again.

"Sampson and I weren't even talking by that point, it was so bad and I was so angry," Dakich said during a 2015 interview. "I called him out on something and told him he was full of shit. So when I got called over to the AD's office, I'm figuring I'm getting fired, figuring Sampson didn't want me around and I was going home.

"I stopped and looked at those banners as I was walking over there and I'm thinking to myself, 'Will I ever see these again?' All those years of playing and coaching under those banners – and all the work that went into those from hundreds of people – and I'm thinking, 'This is how I go out?'

It didn't come to that, of course. Sampson was fired, Dakich was named the interim coach and finished out that season. Crean was hired to clean up Sampson's mess, and life moved forward. It's taken time, but the Hoosiers are back to chasing banners again.

And that's the way it should be. Those banners in a memorable building are something to be proud of, for everyone involved.

"I still live in Bloomington and I pass by Assembly Hall almost every morning on my way to work," Scott May said in a 2015 interview. "When I pass by, I still get this good, good feeling, you know. That's something special, even after all these years."

**PhotoShop Created Image**

The 1975 Hoosiers were ranked No. 1 in the country throughout January and February and dominated the Big Ten at a record-setting pace.

chapter **2**

**W**hen the wins started piling up for the University of Kentucky during the 2014-2015 basketball season – and the Wildcats' loss total stayed stuck at zero – it made for a long winter of stomach churning and teeth gnashing for the loyal Indiana University fan base. Everything we hold sacred was being threatened by those hated one-and-doners to the south.

All the disdain that IU fans hold for the Kentucky program, its fans and – most especially – its coach were on full display. The angst was off the charts, and for good reason. We have all gotten used to UK having No.1-ranked recruiting classes, but during that season they had plenty of holdovers, too. The talk of an undefeated season was kicked around as early as November.

At Indiana, we take great pride in our banners, our history and in doing things right – at least most of the time. But what we've taken the most pride in over the past four decades is that the last college team to finish a season unbeaten, the 1976 Indiana Hoosiers, was ours.

So during Kentucky's run, the spotlight returned to that '76 group of Hoosiers. They did interviews for all the national media and, as always, displayed a lot of class when it looked like their 39-year run was going to finally be matched. We all rooted for Notre Dame against Kentucky anyway in the regional finals and rooted even harder for Wisconsin at the Final Four. And when the Badgers knocked off Kentucky to end their dream season with a 38-and-*ONE* record, IU fans cheered just as hard, as if we had beaten them ourselves.

The streak lived on. Our streak.

The IU unbeaten streak.

But for as great as the 1976 Hoosiers were – they were voted the best college team ever in an NCAA vote in 2013 – and how much we all cherish that magical 32-0 season, there is one undisputable fact that will live on forever.

And it's this: The 1975 Hoosiers were better.

But that team from a year earlier didn't win a national title. They could have, should have and would have. No discussion of missing banners at Indiana can ever begin without first remembering the magic of that 1975 season and how great that team truly was.

In many ways, the 1975 season was even more impressive than 1976. That's saying a lot, considering what the '76 team did hasn't been replicated in 40 years. Quite simply, Indiana could have gone back-to-back as undefeated national champions.

They were that good.

Former Indiana coach Bob Knight has said on many occasions that the '75 group was "the best team I've ever coached." Many of the key pieces of the 1976 team – Scott May, Quinn Buckner, Bobby Wilkerson, Kent Benson, Tom Abernethy – were mainstays in '75 as well, but seniors Steve Green and John Laskowski were also there. Green was one of IU's greatest all-time players. When the forward left IU, he was seventh on the school's all-time scoring list with 1,265 points. Laskowski was so good off the bench that he even graced the cover of Sports Illustrated that season for all he did in his "Super Sub" role.

It was a special group.

"It all came together in a special way," Buckner said. "We had Coach Knight, and there's a reason he's in the Hall of Fame. And we had a terrific group of guys who worked hard every day

24

and played unselfishly every minute of every game."

For the IU fan base – especially those over 40 – we often look at our national championships in bunches. The 1940 and 1953 titles were the ''way-back-in-the-day'' crowns under Branch McCracken, but the 1976, 1981 and 1987 titles under Bob Knight were our current, modern-day titles. The Bob Knight love affair is mostly never-ending for the people who lived through his run.

But back then, as that season started in October of 1974, it really was a different time. "Modern day" and "40 years ago" don't seem to mesh. Some things, over time, we've probably even forgotten. For example:

■ Don't ever forget that Green and Laskowski were the big pieces of Knight's very-first recruiting class at IU after arriving from Army, and May, Buckner and Bobby Wilkerson came to Bloomington a year later. Knight spent 29 years at Indiana, with many moments of greatness tinged with occasional moments of disgust, but back then he was a young 30-something coach just starting to make a big name for himself. But the 29 years of pushing his players, well that never changed. He was always tough, from day one.

"Coach was tough back then, but he always was. That was the Vince Lombardi era, and it was like 'get your butt down, play great defense and work real hard,' " Laskowski said. "He made us believe that we could do more than we could. Practices were not fun. The games were much easier than practice. But when you won, it was all worth it."

■ College basketball was different back then. There was no shot clock, no three-point line, no endless barrage of TV timeouts. There weren't 50 games a night on TV either, though you could almost always find the Hoosiers on game nights if you lived somewhere in Indiana. And despite Knight's reputation as the game's best-ever defensive coach, the '75 IU team could score, oftentimes at will. Their offensive numbers that season were staggering.

"We played a lot of games in the 80s and 90s, even in the hundreds now and then," May said in a recent interview. "We were very efficient on offense and could get scoring from everyone, but a lot of our offense came from our great defense. It led to a lot of fast breaks and a lot of easy layups."

■ Qualifying for the NCAA tournament was also far different from what we know now. IU's 1974 team missed out on the tournament despite being one of the top five or six teams in the country because they didn't win the Big Ten regular season title. Only conference champions made it back then. The following season, it put an enormous amount of pressure on the Hoosiers from the very first practice.

IU Archives P-0020272

Scott May (left) and Quinn Buckner listen intently to instruction from Coach Bob Knight early in the 1974-75 season.

"We weren't about to get stuck in some commissioner's tournament again. We wanted to get back to the NCAAs," May said. "From the first day, we were all about winning the Big Ten, getting into the NCAA tournament, reaching the Final Four and winning it. Anything less was unacceptable. And that was true for all of us."

■ The country was different back then, in the mid-'70s. Civil rights issues and racism were still much-debated topics in several circles. Even though there were no race problems with IU's team – "None. Ever," Buckner said – it doesn't mean they still didn't have to deal with race issues. Their first Big Ten game, for instance, turned into a powder keg at Michigan State when the Spartans' black players refused to play the game because their head coach, Gus Ganakas, refused to start five blacks after his only white starter, Jim Dudley, was injured.

"There were never any black/white things with us," Laskowski said. "There were no cliques at all and we were always all together. We all got along great and we all just pushed each other to work hard and get better all the time. The Michigan State thing, honestly it never even came up in our locker room. We just worried about us. Trust me, we just wanted to survive practice every day."

■ And lastly, even back then, the outside-the-white-lines actions of head coach Bob Knight would play a massively huge role in how this excellent 1975 season would turn out. Yes, greatness and brilliance were back in Bloomington and things happened in the 1975 season that no one had seen at IU in decades. Yes, Bob Knight deserves a lot of credit for that. A whole lot. That will never be questioned.

But this 1975 season ended with just one loss – to the hated University of Kentucky, no less – and Knight can take a share in the blame for that, too. And it had nothing to do with X's

27

and O's or shaky defense.

It had everything to do with a hearty slap to the back of the head of an opposing coach by Knight. It was an embarrassing act where those opposing players vowed revenge in the worst way possible – by beating Indiana when it would hurt the most.

Imagine that.

\*\*\*     \*\*\*     \*\*\*

When the Hoosiers first gathered in the fall of 1974, an immense sense of urgency hung over this team. It was Knight's fourth season in Bloomington and his first recruiting class, led by Green and Laskowski, were now seniors.

Seniors with no rings.

There had been plenty of success, of course, but not the goal of winning a national title. Not yet. There was the pleasant surprise of 1973, when the young Hoosiers shocked the world by beating Marquette and Kentucky in the regionals before losing to No. 1 UCLA in a terrific game at the Final Four. But it was followed by the disappointment of 1974, when the Hoosiers didn't even make the NCAA tournament.

They had been good. Very good, in fact, but they could be better. Knight knew that. The players soon knew it, too.

"It was all about getting the most out of every practice when we started," Buckner said. "Coach Knight talked a lot about how good we were, but that we had to be even that much better the next year. There were areas we could improve in. We worked hard on help defense, worked on being more efficient on offense and we were definitely in better shape. We were definitely ready to go physically."

It was a different time back then. In the '74 season, you

had to win your regular-season conference championship to make the 25-team NCAA field. Indiana was a preseason No. 3 and spent almost the entire season ranked in the top 10. They never fell lower than 13th, and that was only for a week. IU finished the Big Ten season tied with Michigan and was forced to play a playoff game in Champaign, Ill., to determine the conference's representative. The teams split during the regular season, Michigan winning by two in Ann Arbor in January in a game where IU blew a 15-point lead and Indiana winning by 12 in Bloomington in February. Michigan won the playoff game 75-67 and punched their ticket to the NCAAs, where they lost in the regional final to Marquette. IU was relegated to an off-the radar event called the Collegiate Commissioners Association Tournament. Indiana roared through three straight games to claim the title, but it didn't really mean much.

"We had a really good team in '74 but we lost that playoff game to Michigan and didn't make the tournament and that really hurt," Buckner said. "There's no question that pain carried over into the next season. We all came into that '75 season better prepared and we attacked every day early in the year exactly like we needed to. ''

The Hoosiers opened the season ranked No. 3 in the country, behind only defending national champion North Carolina State and perennial power UCLA. Preseason rankings meant nothing to Knight and, frankly, the players didn't care either. They were No. 3 the previous year as well and that didn't turn out the way they wanted. They had only one goal that really mattered at the start of that 1974-75 season and that was to win a national championship.

There was no talk about an undefeated season early in the year, only the talk of a title. That topic wouldn't come until down the road. For the 1975 season, the NCAA field was expanding to 32 teams and a few 'at-large' non-champions were going to get invites. Indiana had no interest in that. They were adamant about winning a Big Ten title.

"After what happened in '74, it was all about being ready every day," May said. "That was kind of stupid, that playoff game with Michigan. Here we are, co-champions of the Big Ten, and we didn't even get into the tournament. It was definitely the stepping stone for the next year."

The day-to-day urgency actually had good reasoning behind it. After an initial cupcake – IU beat Tennessee Tech 113-60 in the biggest season-opening victory in school history – a gauntlet of ranked opponents awaited in a brutal early-season eight-day stretch. There were road games at No. 7 Kansas on Dec. 4 and at No. 11 Notre Dame on Dec. 11, with a home game against No. 15 Kentucky on Dec. 7 sandwiched in between. It was good preparation for the all-important Big Ten schedule, where the winner got the NCAA prize. IU only played three ranked opponents in the 11-game non-conference schedule – and they all came in one grueling week.

It was a week where they would learn a lot about themselves, and the rest of the country would as well.

The Kansas game in Lawrence turned out to be a huge test. The Jayhawks, who had reached the Final Four a year earlier, were very good. They returned four starters and were preseason No. 7 in the Associated Press poll. This was the last of a four-year series between the two legendary basketball schools and the Hoosiers had won the first three. The only two other meetings were to determine national championships. Those banners that hang in Assembly Hall from 1940 and 1953 national championships came with victories over Kansas.

The Hoosiers needed overtime to get past Kansas in Lawrence. They won 74-70 but it was a battle from start to finish. Neither team led by more than seven points the entire night. Kansas shot 55 percent from the field – the best anyone would do against IU all year – and the Hoosiers shot just 42 percent. IU's guards, Quinn Buckner and Bobby Wilkerson, never scored the entire night. Wilkerson took only one shot, a miss, but Bucker was 0-for-8 from the field and also missed the front end of three one-and-ones at the free throw line.

Scott May made up for it. He scored 29 points in what Knight called "the best game he's played since he's been here." He scored the first nine points in overtime for IU and John Laskowski sealed the game with a 15-foot jumper with 42 seconds to go to give Indiana a 71-70 lead.

It was a huge win on the road in a hostile environment.

"That Kansas game was great," Laskowski said. "We beat them in overtime at their place for the second time in three years. They were really good, and it was something to win at Phog Allen Fieldhouse twice."

The win at Notre Dame at week later wasn't as close but it was just as impressive. IU won 94-84, making amends for a home loss a year earlier that turned out to be this group's only career loss at Assembly Hall. Notre Dame was loaded back then. Aside from beating IU the previous year, they had also ended UCLA's record 88-game winning streak.

They had a lot of starters back and had a great scorer in Adrian Dantley, who was averaging 33 points a game at the time. IU played well, leading by as much as 18 in the second half. Steve Green got the call to guard Dantley, and he "held" him to 32 … and came up with one of the best postgame quotes of the year.

"I outslowed him," Green said at the time. "I was about three steps slow, so he would make all those fakes and I'd still be there."

IU Archives P-0039737

Scott May was an exceptional player for Indiana. The 6-foot-8 forward from Sandusky, Ohio was IU's go-to guy on offense in 1975.

The other nonconference games, all against unranked opponents, were nondescript. Every win came by at least 14 points and the average margin of victory in those eight games was 28.4 points. The last three games were in Hawaii, where the Hoosiers won the Rainbow Classic over Christmas break with wins against Florida, Ohio State and Hawaii.

There were a few highlights.

IU beat Texas A&M 90-55 at the ''new'' Market Square Arena in Indianapolis. It was part of a doubleheader with Purdue and the sellout crowd of 17,700 was the largest crowd in the history of Indiana basketball at the time. The Hoosiers also beat a good Toledo team with freshman Wayne Radford playing 24 minutes after Laskowski injured his foot and missed four games. They also won two tournaments, their first Indiana Classic in Bloomington and the Rainbow Classic. They were the first Big Ten team to ever win that event in Hawaii.

But the most important nonconference game with all the drama was the Dec. 7 home game with Kentucky, played in Assembly Hall on a cold Saturday afternoon in early December. There was lots of drama, for many, many reasons.

***    ***    ***

There have been many times through the years when greatness has crossed paths in the Kentucky-Indiana rivalry. December of 1974 did not seem to be one of those times.

Indiana had their unquestioned coach of the future in Knight, without a shred of doubt. Kentucky wasn't so sure with Joe B. Hall. Hall was hired to replace the legendary UK coach Adolph Rupp in 1972 but things weren't going well for Hall in Lexington. He was 20-8 his first year but was only 13-13 in 1974 and he had a

33

near mutiny on his hands.

There were many powerful UK boosters – and powerful is probably too mild an adjective in horse country – who wanted Hall fired at all costs. He was in that much trouble.

"Hall got the job (after Rupp) under some controversial circumstances and a lot of people didn't like it. Even Rupp came to resent him," said Billy Reed, the legendary longtime writer and columnist in Lexington and Louisville who also wrote college basketball and other things for Sports Illustrated for decades. He's been around the UK-IU rivalry for 50 years. "Some UK alums, they handed him the job after Rupp. Hall's first year, he went 20-8 with this great group of sophomores but IU beat them to go to the Final Four there in 1973. But then the next year he went 13-13 and he was definitely on the hot seat after that. Everyone thought they should be much better than they were.

"There's no question he was in big trouble. He was about to get run out of town, it was that bad."

So here strides Hall and his Wildcats into Assembly Hall, possibly one embarrassment away from getting the boot for good. Knight, who had been a fishing buddy of Hall's through the years and considered him a friend, was already 3-0 against him. Knight had also beaten Rupp in his first year at IU, so he was a perfect 4-0 against a Kentucky program "he had always been fascinated with" as a youngster, Reed said.

"It goes all the way back to when he was a kid growing up in Orrville, Ohio," Reed said. "Back in those days, Kentucky was the premier program and Knight was just fascinated with Rupp. He told me he would listen to Kentucky games on the radio on WHAS back in the '50s. He played in the UKIT (holiday tournament) when he coached at Army and his first year at Indiana was Rupp's last year at Kentucky. He beat Rupp that first year (90-89 in double

34

overtime at Freedom Hall in Louisville) and I know that really meant a lot to him."

Hall had been Rupp's assistant for years and it was during that time he and Knight had become friends. They were heading in different directions for sure when the December 1974 game rolled around. Knight was building a monster team; Hall was halfway out the door.

And then, to make matters worse, the Hoosiers ripped them a new one.

"That Kentucky game, we really jumped out on them," May said. "It's too bad that rivalry is in the toilet now, because it was huge back then, especially for the Indiana people. I was from Ohio, but I caught on very quickly as to how important that game was. We got after them, and as I remember we made everything. It was one of those home games where you got rolling and just fed off the crowd. We played great."

IU guards Quinn Buckner and Bobby Wilkerson – still considered by many the best defensive backcourt in college basketball history – simply took over the game. They bothered UK stars Jimmy Dan Connor, Mike Flynn and Kevin Grevey so much that they not only couldn't get good looks, but they could barely possess the ball. Indiana's half-court defense was that tough.

"They were a machine. They kicked our ass bad," Kentucky senior guard Mike Flynn said in a 2015 interview. Flynn was the 1971 Indiana Mr. Basketball from Jeffersonville. "They made everything and our freshmen big guys, man they got overwhelmed by (Kent) Benson. We really struggled to score. They had our number for a while there.

"We couldn't play on the varsity as freshmen but we played Indiana's freshmen at Freedom Hall and won. But on the varsity I lost to them every time. They beat us at home and in

Bloomington and beat us in the Elite Eight in '73."

Benson was unstoppable. He had a career-high 26 points and 12 rebounds against UK's freshmen centers. He scored 11 straight points in just over two minutes in the big second-half run and delivered a shivering forearm to the teeth of UK freshman Rick Robey while battling for position down low, popped hard in he face just as he was the previous year as a freshman in this intense and physical rivalry.

At one point late in the second half, IU had a 34-point lead. IU destroyed Kentucky's passive 1-3-1 zone all day. Knight called off the dogs with more than eight minutes to go, taking out all his starters with a rousing 33-point lead. They were that good. Knight gushed over their performance.

"I feel about as good about our play in the first 10 to 12 minutes as I have about any since I've been here," he said.

But in the final minute of the game, the always-volatile Knight walked all the way down in front of the Kentucky bench to yell at the referees, Flynn said. He railed and railed, and when he was finished, Hall said to his fishing friend, "Give him hell, Bob."

Knight went nuts. He started yelling at Hall for talking to him during a game, even though it was over for all intents and purposes. Hall considered his comment harmless. But the infuriated Knight went on and on and when he was finished he cuffed Hall in the back of the head. UK assistant Lynn Nance, who was a former FBI agent, jumped off the bench and got right after Knight before they were separated by officials. The chaos lasted for several minutes.

When the game ended, Hall refused to shake Knight's hand. Knight, of course, refused to admit he did anything wrong. After all, Knight presumed, there was nothing wrong with what he did. He had done the same thing with his own players many times, he said. Knight didn't consider a head slap to be a problem. The friendship basically ended right there on the spot.

"That altercation with Hall, Knight slapping him in the head, was just adding insult to injury as far as the UK fans were concerned," Reed said. "But as angry as they had become with Hall, now they directed all their anger at Knight. They didn't like him anyway; thought he was a bully.

"But that one moment changed everything. If Knight doesn't slap him, who knows what happens to Hall. He might have been fired that week, as angry as a lot of those big boosters were. It could have happened. Instead, everyone seemed to rally around it. The seniors just took over that team and they weren't going to put up with being embarrassed anymore. They beat North Carolina and Kansas and Notre Dame right after that and then they ran through the SEC pretty easily except for a few little bobbles at the end. They had become a very good team after that day that Knight hit Hall. And that game against IU, it looked like they couldn't beat anybody."

The Hall slap didn't affect the IU players in any way, of course. "I don't remember it, and it was never even discussed at the time," May said recently. "It never came up in our locker room, not even once."

But it changed the UK players in an instant, especially the Indiana kids on the UK roster who took it personally. The incident came up in their locker room all the time. Flynn, after all, was a Jeffersonville native who was the 1971 Indiana Mr. Basketball and had spurned Knight's first-year recruiting efforts. They were angry ... and all the anger was directed at Knight.

"He was walking away and he cuffed Coach Hall right upside the head. We all saw it and, man, we were all angry. What he did there really left a bad taste in our mouths," Flynn said. "I tell ya, that really woke us up. We wound up having a great year but all the time we were watching Indiana. We wanted a rematch so bad. We were out for revenge, especially me because I was a senior and it was my last shot. Coach Knight made a big mistake popping Coach Hall that night. He was a great coach and all, but I didn't respect him one bit. Not after that."

All Flynn and his Wildcats teammates wanted was another chance to play Indiana … and to stick it to Knight. That one slap brought them together and changed their lackluster ways.

The slap, it meant nothing to Knight. Of course it wouldn't.

It meant everything to those Kentucky players.

# Chapter 3

When the calendar turned to 1975, the Hoosiers were 11-0 and ranked No. 2 in the country behind N.C. State, the '74 champs who also were still undefeated. Neither the record nor the ranking really mattered much to the players, who were still totally focused on that "get better every day" mantra that IU coach Bob Knight preached so hard.

It was also time for the Big Ten season to start and that was all that really mattered to the Hoosiers. Even though the NCAA tournament was expanding from 25 to 32 teams for the first time, IU players had no interest in taking any chances with a selection committee. Their goal was to win the Big Ten and be guaranteed a spot.

Simple enough.

As usual, the Big Ten was deep and competitive. IU was favored, of course, but there would be battles, especially on the road. For the first time, the Big Ten – which was still 10 teams back then – would play a complete round-robin schedule, everyone twice, once at home and once on the road.

It would be a grind, one surely able to produce a most-deserving champion. Indiana expected that trophy to come their way, and the first trip of the year – tough games on a Saturday and Monday against a good Michigan State team and Michigan, their nemesis from the year before – was going to be huge.

It turned out to be the most bizarre four days of the season, and mostly for events off the court.

*** *** ***

**Christmas break was still** going on and the IU campus was basically empty on the Friday the team was preparing to fly to Michigan. Because all the other dorms and fraternities were closed during the break, the players all stayed at the Eigenmann Residence Center on campus until school reopened on Monday.

No problem, right? Well …

"That was such an important trip for us and it almost never happened," Laskowski said recently. "It's Friday afternoon and we're getting ready to leave to take the bus from Assembly Hall to the airport and they tell us we have to move out of our rooms before we leave because all the regular students would be coming back before we got back home. We all grabbed our stuff but (Quinn) Buckner, (Scott) May, (Bobby) Wilkerson and Jim Wisman had just gotten back to the dorm and didn't have enough time to move out. So they're hurrying to grab all their stuff and they call the basketball office. They get some manager and tell him they're going to be late but he never tells Coach Knight.

"So it's 2 o'clock and most of us are on the bus and it's time to go. A few minutes go by and Coach Knight says 'Ok, let's go.' He's ready to leave without them. That was one of his few rules, that you could never be late. Well, (assistant coach Dave) Bliss says to wait and he gets off the bus. The bus leaves without him. He goes over to the dorm to find out what's going on. They tell him about having to move out and he thinks it's a legitimate excuse and gets the guys and they drive like crazy to the airport.

"Their car shows up and we're already on the plane. Coach Bliss is trying to explain what happened to Coach Knight but he doesn't want anything to do with it. He's yelling at them,

40

yelling at Coach Bliss, yelling like only Coach Knight can, if you know what I mean. He's like 'All five of you aren't going,' even Coach Bliss.

"Well, finally, the pilot comes out and he tells Coach Knight that he has a list of who is supposed to be on the plane and FAA rules say that if those five people on the list don't get on the plane, then they can't take off until he gets a new list. Coach finally let them on the plane and we took off, but he was still mad about it.

"Can you imagine that? Our biggest road trip of the year and we almost took off without three of our starters?"

Saved by FAA regulations.

Michigan State was first up. The Spartans were tough and talented, and always difficult to beat in the old Jenison Fieldhouse, a small, dingy facility that could get very loud. But just hours before the Saturday game, one of the darkest moments in Michigan State basketball history took place and it led to one of the weirdest games in Big Ten history.

Jim Dudley was the only white starter on that Michigan State team. Four blacks started and the first two players usually off the bench were black players too. But when Michigan State coach Gus Ganakas told his team on the afternoon of the game that fresh-man Jeff Tropf – one of two other white players on the team – was going to make his first career start for the injured Dudley, the black players got the message.

Ganakas wasn't about to start five black players.

Maybe that doesn't matter now, but in 1975 it sure did. The 10 black players on the team were so upset that they walked out of the fieldhouse. They came back a few hours later, but Ganakas suspended them all anyway.

So when the game started against mighty Indiana, Tropf and a bunch of junior varsity players took the court. As expected,

41

IU Archives P-0055994
Kent Benson (54) was a sophomore at Indiana during the 1975 season
and he was a handful for opposing centers, especially with his hook shot.

it was an embarrassing whitewash, with the Hoosiers winning 107-55 and the 10 suspended players watching from the stands. To this day, it remains the worst loss in Big Ten history for the Spartans. It was, at the time, also the largest margin of victory in a Big Ten game for IU, but that record wouldn't last long.

For the Indiana players, black and white, they simply stayed true to the task at hand. They went in and won a basketball game and went on with their season. That was that.

"We talked about it briefly, but not for long," Indiana guard and team leader Quinn Buckner said of Michigan State's race-based walkout and the subsequent player suspensions. "It was their situation, not ours, and it was our job to be prepared to play and take care of what we could control. That's what we did. Our conversation was that this was their thing and it had nothing to do with Indiana basketball. We left it at that."

Buckner said the topic of race was never an issue at Indiana and what went on at Michigan State didn't affect them in any way, then or ever.

"We had no black/white issues ever. Not one," he said. "Coach Knight preached to us all the time about being a team and even though a lot of us came from different circumstances, we all got along so well. We bonded together well and with us, it was always more about the group pulling for the group."

Buckner shared a story of a similar situation he went through while at Thornridge High School in south suburban Chicago. He learned then that it wasn't his place to speak up on the issue, and he wasn't about to do it at Michigan State either.

"I had dealt with a situation like that before in high school. It was a predominately white school and a friend's sister, who was black, didn't make the varsity cheerleading team and she should have. I had a discussion with my father about it and he said that when there's nothing you can do about it, then be careful what you say about it. I learned from that."

All that mattered at the time was that the Hoosiers were 1-0 and two days away from playing Michigan, its arch-rival at the time and the team that had ruined IU's season a year earlier.

*** *** ***

**O**n the afternoon of the first IU-Michigan matchup, the Hoosiers got some good news. Thanks to an N.C. State loss over the weekend, the Associated Press poll now had the Hoosiers ranked as the No. 1 team in the land. It was a first time an IU team had been ranked No. 1 since late 1954, a span of nearly 21 years.

If it seems like a long drought at No. 1 for an IU team, it's because it is. It's the longest gap between top rankings since the polls started. Not *was* the longest gap, *is* the longest gap still to this day.

But you have to remember, this was indeed a different time. For years, the Hoosiers weren't even winning Big Ten titles. When Knight's second team at IU won the Big Ten in 1973, it was the first time in 15 years that the Hoosiers had won a conference title outright, and there was even only one co-championship (1967) in there. Before the '73 Final Four run, the Hoosiers hadn't won a meaningful NCAA Tournament game since winning the 1953 national championship. (They did win two regional tournament consolation games in 1954 and 1958 after semifinal losses to Notre Dame, but those clearly were irrelevant wins.)

Against ranked opponents in that two-decade downturn, IU was only 20-43. Shocking, isn't it?

So being No. 1 again, yes it was nice. But it also didn't matter much. There were bigger goals still ahead.

44

"I don't want to minimize what these kids have accomplished, but it's kind of like watching the previews and the cartoon before the feature at the movies," Knight said at the time. "The feature is March."

Since the previous March without an NCAA tournament bid had hurt so much, it was nice to go to Michigan and win 90-76 later that night. The 17th-ranked Wolverines had lost a few people from their '74 team, but they were still very good. The road win was huge.

"It was really good to beat them and make a statement, especially after what had happened the previous year," Buckner said. "We were very focused that night and really played well. It was a good trip to start the Big Ten season."

In Indiana's home opener on Saturday, Jan. 11, the Hoosiers completely dismantled Iowa and won 102-49. Their record for largest Big Ten win at Michigan State had lasted exactly one week. IU's defense was so suffocating that Iowa didn't even get a shot off on its first five possessions, which all ended with turnovers. The Hoosiers were now 14-0 and had won 17 straight games dating back to 1974, the longest winning streak in school history … at the time.

IU beat Minnesota at home 79-59 two nights later, showing off perfection in another way. They led only 56-53 in the second half before running away with the game and didn't make a single turnover in the final 20 minutes. The Hoosiers were making it look much easier than it really was.

The following Saturday, Indiana traveled to Northwestern for a night game that was way too late at night for Knight. The Hoosiers won 82-56, but Knight thumbed his nose at the conference and its TV partners for having to play so late, even on a weekend night, to satisfy the TV people.

"It was ridiculous. I guarantee you it won't happen in Bloomington," Knight said at the time. "If we've got a game scheduled for 4:05, it's going to start at 4:05, regardless of the repercussions."

That, of course, was typical Knight. He liked things his way and hated anyone upsetting his routine. He craved complete focus from his players and complete control of his program.

This was, after all, just his fourth year in Bloomington and Knight was still a very young 34 years old. Even dealing with being No. 1 in the polls rankled him. He was never critical of his players, just the circus that started to emerge around being the top team in the country. He wasn't much for the media demands, especially from the media idiots he didn't think knew anything.

"Right now our players can look at it as a sense of accomplishment, but I'm not sure it's even that big of a deal to our play-

IU Arcives P-0055940
Bob Knight watches from one knee during a game at Assembly Hall in the 1975 season. The plaid jackets were in back then.

ers," Knight said then. "Here you are, rated first, and a guy calls and doesn't know the names of your players or who you play next.

"I could tell him how we've won with a combination of zone defenses or make up names – which I haven't done, although I've been tempted – because I know it's just something they're doing now and as soon as you get beat they're going to go on to the next guy."

The media wasn't going to go away anytime soon. The Hoosiers were playing too well and their domination of the Big Ten was becoming relentless.

In their 89-69 win over Wisconsin two nights later, the Hoosiers once again displayed how in-tune they were, especially on offense. Buckner made 13 of 14 shots, the best mark in the Big Ten in four years, and Scott May extended his free throw streak to 27 in a row before finally missing.

IU was now 17-0 and 6-0 in the conference, with No. 20-ranked Purdue next up in Bloomington on Saturday, Jan. 25. Like most years, IU and Purdue really mattered. They came into the season considered to be the two best teams in the Big Ten. Even though it was Michigan who got the NCAA bid in '74, it was IU and Purdue who both won postseason tournaments (CCA and NIT, respectively) the previous year.

If anyone could derail IU's unbeaten season, it seems as though Purdue had the best chance, especially since IU senior forward Steve Green missed the game with the flu. But the Hoosiers dismissed those thoughts immediately, trouncing their in-state rivals to the north 104-71. John Laskowski started for Green and they didn't miss a beat. All five starters scored in double figures to push their record to 18-0. The 18 straight wins in a season broke the school record of the 1953 team, which had won 17 in a row.

Beating Purdue, as always, was nice. It was another statement game for IU.

"Purdue, obviously, was a major rival, and it was good to really play a great game against them," Buckner said. "I wasn't from Indiana so I didn't understand the intensity of that rivalry at first, but I sure caught on right away. Every game with them was huge. And Ohio State was big too, being Coach Knight's alma mater and all. But even against a team like Northwestern, that maybe didn't have as much talent as we did, we still prepared for them just has hard. That's what I always admired about Coach Knight. He had us ready for every single game. We never got a game ahead. The way we prepared, every game was a big game. Every win was nice. The rivalry games too. But beating Purdue was always fun because we could tell how much it meant to everyone else, too."

Indiana beat Illinois 73-57 for its 19th win despite not shooting well, and win No. 20 would be much harder. Next up was Ohio State in Columbus. Knight, who was a reserve guard on the great Ohio State teams of the early 1960s with John Lucas and John Havlicek, had never won as a coach in Columbus, losing once when he came there with one of his Army teams and all three times as coach at IU.

Ohio State had the luxury – if you could call it that – of already having some experience with this loaded IU team. They met in Hawaii in December in the semifinals of the Rainbow Classic. IU won 102-71 in a rout, but the experience was good for the Buckeyes nonetheless. They felt like they had a chance at home, especially considering history. They had beaten IU in Columbus eight straight times, including a win in 1974 that kept IU from passing Michigan in the Big Ten race. And IU wasn't 100 percent themselves. Green was back from the flu, but Bobby Wilkerson had been hit in the eye with a ball during practice and there was some question as to how effective he might be.

The game was nip and tuck the whole way, with IU finally prevailing 72-66. Wilkerson played, but wasn't at his best. Buckner hurt his knee midway through the game and played through it. Each possession was a grind. IU was glad to get out of town with a win. To be 20-0, it sounded pretty good.

"They are a very tough ballclub for us. That was the toughest game we've been in for some time," Knight said after the game. "I'd say we got a pretty good test tonight. I'm not big on getting any better test."

Buckner's knee swelled up pretty bad the next day and he missed a few practices. He was back for the Michigan rematch though, and played well in a 74-48 rout. Michigan tried to stall – remember, no shot clock back in those days – but it didn't work. Wilkerson had a season-high 18 points and the game was never close. He and Buckner were stifling on defense, once again earning more praise as the best defensive backcourt in the country.

It was a title they cherished. Both had been prolific scorers in high school but changed their games for the greater good at Indiana.

"Hey, when you're playing with Scott May and Steve Green – and later Kent Benson – you really don't need to be a scoring threat," Buckner said. "We all came there as a highly touted group with different skill sets. But we all bought in to what needed to be done as a team. I was a scorer in high school, but I gave up a lot of that game to focus on getting the ball to the right guys and playing great defense every possession. I had a football coach in high school who said 'If you score, you may win but if you defend well you will always win.' That was my mindset at Indiana, and that never changed."

It was the same with Wilkerson. He was a prolific scorer at

Anderson Madison Heights High School before coming to Indiana. But his grades weren't good and he had to sit out his freshman year at IU as a "non-predictor," a term used back in those days for student-athletes who needed to first prove themselves in the classroom before they could play. But that year of not playing helped. He assimilated to Bloomington well and saw what he needed to do to help the team when he finally came on board for the 1974 season. He and Buckner were beasts on the defensive end.

"I came here with one attitude, but I had to change to concentrate on only one thing – defense," Wilkerson said at the time. There were some games where he'd go a half at a time without even getting a shot off, but "I didn't even worry about that. I knew my job."

IU reeled off four more easy wins to get to 25-0 before its rematch with Purdue. The Hoosiers beat Iowa 79-56, and the Hawkeyes shot just 29 percent from the field. They had shot only 26 percent in the first meeting. IU won at Minnesota 69-54 then came home to beat Northwestern 82-58. Buckner was exceptional, leading a ball-hawking defense that helped IU rush out to a 48-16 halftime lead. Knight gave him the ultimate compliment afterward.

"He's just got a great basketball mind, as fine a basketball mind as anyone I've ever been around," Knight said of his leader.

IU trounced Wisconsin 93-58 for win No. 25 and No. 14 in the conference, clinching at least a tie for the Big Ten title with four games to go. The Hoosiers had won or a shared a Big Ten title for the third year in a row, which was the first time that had been done in school history. Buckner and his classmates won the conference the following year also in 1976, so a clean sweep was nice.

"The Big Ten was tough. In retrospect, winning the title was the goal from the beginning, not going undefeated," Buckner said. "But being part of four straight Big Ten championship teams was something to be proud of. ''

Winning the title outright with a win at Purdue was the next goal, but it wasn't going to be easy. Now the injury bug had caught up to sophomore center Kent Benson, who was missing practice time with back spasms. He was the fourth of five starters to miss workouts in the past month. Only leading scorer Scott May had been healthy the whole time.

IU's history in West Lafayette wasn't very good either. The Hoosiers had never won – yes, never – in the new Mackey Arena, losing their first five games there. Here's an even more amazing stat: In the previous 20 years, Indiana had only won *one time* in West Lafayette.

It was time for that to change, even if they were fighting through some aches and pains.

"We had some injuries along the way that season but we were always good at fighting through them," Buckner said. "I had a minor issue with my knee but it wasn't about to stop me from playing basketball. I was a football guy, and I knew what it was like to be banged up. You weren't going to keep me out of a basketball game.

"And as far as Coach Knight went, he never talked about injuries at all. We just worked hard every day with whoever was there. We had plenty of depth anyway and whether it was me or Steve (Green) or Kent with his back, or John with his foot, we just got after it every day."

Practices were crisp and intense leading up to the Purdue game. They were prepared, and ready to clinch the Big Ten title and the NCAA berth that went with it. There was plenty of excitement in the air.

It was going to be a very special night.

It turned out to be ... but for all the wrong reasons.

51

Quinn Buckner (21) had a great reputation as a defensive stopper, but he could also take the ball to the basket when he had to.

\*\*\*    \*\*\*    \*\*\*

It seemed like nothing at the time. Scott May felt a pain in his left forearm and he wasn't even sure how he hurt it early in the first half of IU's showdown with Purdue in West Lafayette. He even went back into the game and battled hard against the hated Boilermakers.

"At Purdue, I got a stress fracture first. That feels like getting stuck with a needle," May said. "It hurt, but I kept playing and then I got hit again a little later. That's when it probably got broken."

May scored eight points, but the pain never went away. A trip to the hospital for X-rays found a broken forearm. His team-mates carried on in his absence.

"When Scott went down, it was no different from some-one spraining an ankle in a lot of ways," Buckner said. "It's still a game and you still need to play. You still have to execute on the next possession, so just go do it."

And execute they did. Indiana scored 50 first-half points but still couldn't shake the Boilermakers, leading by only four at the half in front of a raucous sellout crowd of 14,123 at Mackey Arena. Steve Green was on fire for IU, making his first 11 shots from the field and 13 of 15 overall, scoring 29 points.

IU center Kent Benson, who had battled through back issues all week, added 18 points and a season-high 14 rebounds. IU ran out to a six-point lead a few times in the second half, but Purdue always battled back. There were eight ties in the final eight minutes, the last coming at 80-all with less than three minutes to go. Green scored to break the tie, then hit one of two free throws after IU held the ball for more than a minute to go up 83-80. Purdue scored and then had two more chances to win after Buckner lost the ball when he tripped coming up the court with 11 seconds left. Wilkerson made two huge defensive plays and his last deflection forced the ball into Buckner's hands. He tossed it down to the other end of the court as time expired and the Hoosiers escaped with an 83-82 victory.

"We didn't know the severity of Scott's injury until after the game," Buckner said. "We had a fight on our hands with Purdue anyway and we had just lost our best scorer. But still, you just figure out what to do next and go forward. That's how Coach prepared us anyway. When somebody went out, there was always another play to be made. That's what we did."

It took everything they had to secure that 26th victory and clinch the Big Ten title outright. With May out and Laskowski in, the Hoosiers played the entire second half with just five guys. Even Benson, who was fighting through back pain, played the entire second half.

Every possession mattered and Knight played it as such. For the entire second half, it was all Buckner, Wilkerson, May, Benson and Laskowski.

It said something about the importance of that night, playing only five guys, especially since IU had won in West Lafayette only once in the previous 21 years.

But it also sent up a bit of a red flag.

If IU had so much depth, then why was Knight trying to win with only five guys?

**W**ith their primary regular-season goal accomplished, all that remained prior to the NCAA tournament were three league games. The first was at Illinois, two nights after May's broken arm at Purdue, followed by home games to end the season with Ohio State and Michigan State.

Back then the NCAA tourney bracket worked differently as well. Having already clinched the Big Ten, IU knew exactly where it would be playing in the tournament. There was no glitzy "Selection Sunday" show back then, simply an automatic slot in the field based on winning the league. IU would play a first-round game against a yet-undetermined at-large opponent in Lexington, Ky., before moving on – hopefully – to the Midwest regional in Dayton, Ohio.

But first there was work to be done ... and decisions to be made.

The work: Continuing to build on its potential, even without May, and sealing the deal on an undefeated season, which was now suddenly very close.

"Going undefeated, we never really thought about it that way all season long. It was win or lose each night; it was that simple," Buckner said. "For us, it was all about playing up to our potential. We felt when we did that, all the wins and losses would take care of themselves."

Even Knight was willing to share in the undefeated talk by then. "I think, without question, it would be a hell of an honor for these kids to go unbeaten," he said. "But the important thing is to keep playing. If you start relaxing on some things, I've always thought you never get back to where you were."

And, of course, the decisions: With May out of the starting lineup, Knight had to come up with a new plan. There was one obvious choice, moving senior Super Sub John Laskowski into the starting lineup at May's forward spot. But Knight also could play Laskowski at guard and slide Wilkerson down to forward for better defensive matchups as necessary. Or he could leave Laskowski in his vaunted sixth-man role and start Tom Abernethy at forward or go instead with a guard – either Jim Crews, Jim Wisman or Wayne Radford – and leave Laskowski off the bench and Wilkerson at forward.

He had options. And three games to know for sure before the NCAAs.

When the game started at Illinois, it was Laskowski who got the call.

"After Scott got hurt on a Saturday at Purdue we bussed to Illinois for our next game on a Monday night," Laskowski said. "When we practiced Sunday – a day later – Coach told me he was going to start me and I was going to play at the top of the key against their zone. This was one day after we lost Scott – our best player – and Coach had already devised a plan.

"With one day to work on it, I score 18 in the first half and score 28 overall, my career high, and we beat them. That was the genius of Coach, and the mind he had. He made a big adjustment like that on the fly and we didn't miss a beat offensively."

Laskowski was 11 of 13 shooting and had nine rebounds and nine assists in the first start as IU won 112-89. Steve Green added 30 and Kent Benson had 20 as the Hoosiers shot 57 percent in an offensive masterpiece. Knight summed up Laskowski's night accurately and succinctly. "I'd say he responded to the challenge pretty well," Knight said.

The final two home games were a bit of a coronation. IU beat Ohio State 86-78 on Saturday, March 1 and beat Michigan State 94-79 a week later to finish the regular season 29-0. They got battles from both of them.

Knight only used six players in the Ohio State win, a game that stayed within single digits most of the way. Always one to prefer rest over practice come tournament time, IU only practiced for 40 minutes on Thursday and just 15 minutes on Friday before the Michigan State game. 'We're tired," Knight said.

Michigan State gave them a fight. The Spartans had something to prove after not being able to play against IU in the Big Ten opener two months earlier because of a race-related walkout and eventual suspension. They were ready, even jumping out to a 10-point lead midway through the first half before IU ripped off a 45-19 run. Knight said, "We haven't played any better all year than the last 13 minutes of the first half."

The Michigan State game ended with seniors Green and Laskowski leaving to a roaring ovation from the Assembly Hall faithful, replaced by fellow seniors Doug Allen and John Kamstra. The fifth senior from Knight's first IU recruiting class, Steve Ahlfeldt, had come in earlier. It was a special night for the five of them – and Knight.

This first class was special, above and simply beyond being the first class. They had christened Assembly Hall together, shared great things with Knight and were totally embraced by a rabid fan base thrilled to be back among the college basketball elite. Knight, who had started an unofficial tradition of honoring seniors on that night during his first season, asked the crowd to stick around after the final game so he could say a few words to honor the seniors.

IU Archives P-0055941

Indiana's games with Kentucky were incredibly physical during the 1974-75 season, as Steve Green (34) can attest. He got hit in the head with both arms during the IU-UK game in Bloomington.

It's an etched-in-stone tradition we take for granted now. Senior Night basically started with Knight, and on a March Saturday in 1975 it was Knight's first class to say goodbye.

"You always have a special affinity for the first group you work with," Knight said at the time. "They have been through the thick and the thin and they have been a part of everything, even that first year when they couldn't play on the varsity (the last year freshmen weren't eligible.) There's no way you could ever find five who could have worked harder or been more competitive than those five."

They left Assembly Hall for the last time with a 29-0 overall record, a perfect 18-0 mark in the Big Ten and a No. 1 ranking. It was a special season. Only one other Big Ten team in the past 56 years – the 1961 Ohio State team that Knight was a part of as a player – had finished a league season without a blemish. They had won their Big Ten games by a whopping 22.8 points per game, the best ever. Their 51.2 shooting percentage was the best in school history. In their three years at Assembly Hall, the seniors went 36-1 in their new home, losing only to Notre Dame in the 1973-74 season.

"That was one of the most impressive things we did during those two years (1975 and 1976), winning every Big Ten game. To win every road game for two years was amazing," May said. "It's hard to win on the road in the Big Ten because you're their Final Four every game. Everyone gave us their best shot and we answered the bell every time."

Surviving the Big Ten unscathed was impressive. Next up was carrying a target on their backs as the favorite heading into the NCAA Tournament. It would start in a week, against Texas-El Paso in the first round of the Mideast Regional.

They were ready, even without May. They proved a lot to

themselves in those last three Big Ten games without him.

"I started the rest of the Big Ten games and we won them all, even without the best player in the country," Laskowski said. "We all had so much respect for Scott, but we also knew we could still be a real good team without him."

*** *** ***

**Down in Lexington**, the University of Kentucky Wildcats paid attention to their NCAA draw as well. After finishing the season with a 21-4 record and another Southeastern Conference championship, the Wildcats were being dispatched to Tuscaloosa, Ala., for its first-round game against Marquette. Their season had turned out well after all the bad vibes from early in the season, and despite a few hiccups on the road as the SEC schedule wound down, they were ready for the NCAA tournament to begin.

And then they started checking out the bracket.

They could see it plain as day. Beat Marquette in the opener, beat the Central Michigan-Georgetown winner in the second round and then look forward to seeing No. 1-ranked Indiana in the Mideast Regional final in Dayton.

Indiana-Kentucky, one more time. That's all the Wildcats wanted. They had wanted it since being embarrassed in Bloomington on Dec. 7, wanted revenge so badly. And for the Wildcats, that rematch was now just two games away.

"We knew we would be playing them again," UK's Mike Flynn said. "I would watch them on TV whenever I was home in Jeffersonville. One time, Coach Hall and (assistant coach Dick) Parsons drove over and we all watched an Indiana game on TV together at my father-in-law's house. It's was kind of fun, all of us just sitting there in his living room, watching the game and taking notes.

"When the time came, we were going to be ready."

\*\*\*   \*\*\*   \*\*\*

**F**or the Hoosiers, the first foe of the tournament was the Texas-El Paso Miners, a team they were very familiar with. They had played two years earlier in a holiday tournament in El Paso – and Indiana lost.  Knight and UTEP coach Don Haskins were good friends who fished together often. They were a tough defensive-minded team … but one that also respected Indiana's defensive skills.

"Buckner and Wilkerson, they can set one-man traps," said Haskins, whose team lived in the Top 20 most every year back then and had won the 1966 NCAA title when they were known as Texas Western. (The movie "Glory Road" was about their hisoric title run.)

He proved prophetic. Indiana won 78-52. IU's defense was great all day but the offense really struggled to get off to a good start. An 11 a.m. tipoff didn't help – again a TV decision that Knight didn't like – and the Hoosiers shot only 33 percent in the first half, a season low.

Scott May, with his left arm heavily bandaged, played the final 51 seconds. With the win, the Hoosiers raised their record to 30-0 and their 33-game winning streak became a new Big Ten record.

With the NCAA field now down to 16, the field was set for the Mideast Regional in Dayton. The semifinals would be Oregon State against Indiana and Kentucky against Central Michigan. Oregon State had a positive history with Indiana, as well. The Beavers had beaten Indiana 61-48 in the Far West Classic during

61

the 1974 season and came into this game respecting the Hoosiers, but not fearing them.

Being 30-0 or not, Knight knew Oregon State would be ready for them.

"The games that we have played are over. I don't think it makes a difference to anybody what their record is now," Knight said then.

Oregon State coach Ralph Miller agreed.

"My people are in a fortunate situation. This is a team we have met before," he said. "No. 1 in the country doesn't really mean anything to us. I happen to be in a league where we've played a No. 1 team (UCLA) many times before. No. 1 doesn't awe us. We played them. We're going to play this game, too."

It had been an odd week for the Hoosiers. Knight was sick with the flu most of the week and was seen at practice each day but that was it. May practiced every day, but gingerly. And everyone practiced gingerly around him and his still-broken forearm.

"I don't think he's at a situation where you can say, 'All right, he'll play now.' " Knight said then. "A lot depends on the game situations and what we have to do defensively and what we have to do against their defense."

Turns out, they didn't need him. IU ran away from Oregon State 81-71, with Green leading the way with 34 points in an impressive showing. Benson added 23.

"Those first two games, we played really well," Laskowski said. We were playing with a lot of confidence. With or without Scott, we still had the same goals and we still felt very good about accomplishing them."

\*\*\*　　\*\*\*　　\*\*\*

It had been 105 days since Indiana had embarrassed Kentucky in its regular-season showdown and for 105 days the 'Cats had wanted revenge. Their anger of getting blown out and then having their coach, Joe B. Hall, get slapped in the back of the head by Knight had festered every day into all-out hatred.

They wanted Indiana bad and UK came to Dayton with confidence that they could beat the Hoosiers.

"Kentucky was so much better in March than they were in December. All their young kids had really grown up," legendary Kentucky sports columnist Billy Reed said in a recent interview. "And their seniors, well they really wanted to go out in style. By March, Kentucky was not only a very good team, but they were also deep, too."

Since May's injury, Indiana's bench had become very short. With Super Sub John Laskowski starting, only Tom Abernethy was seeing any serious time off the bench in tight situations. Sometimes that didn't even happen. After May's injury at Purdue, Knight played only Green, Benson, Laskowski, Buckner and Wilkerson the entire 20 minutes of the second half.

These were, 105 days later, certainly two different teams.

"When Indiana had Scott May, even then they didn't have a deep bench, I didn't think, but they had five starters with very defined roles and they were very, very good," Reed said. "There's no question they were the best team in the country. But when May went out, they changed. No disrespect to John Laskowski in any way, because he had some good games when May was out, but it wasn't the same, especially on defense.

"Look, I'm sure over time people have forgotten how great a player Scott May was, or maybe they never knew. But those few years, he was great. He was player of the year in the country for good reason the next year, he was that good."

Come tipoff time on March 22, Knight had a decision to make about May. He was nowhere near recovered from the broken bone in his left forearm, but he was practicing anyway. He could not wear a cast in the game, so the medical folks wrapped his arm in thick foam padding so he could play.

"I came back to practice; that was Coach's idea. He wanted me to see if I could withstand the pain," May said. "Once I could start to catch the ball, I started practicing more, because it was my off-arm after all. But it wasn't going to work out. It wasn't good. But I tried. I tried."

Knight put him in the starting lineup, figuring he needed as many shooters in the game as possible against Kentucky's zone. He got seven minutes out of him, and that was it. May made his first shot but missed three others. The pace of the game was quick and it was very physical. Bodies were flying everywhere.

IU Archives P-0055943

Referees had to separate Bob Knight and Kentucky coach Joe B. Hall after an incident in the regular season game. Knight angered UK players.

"The Kentucky game, it was really physical. I only played a few minutes," May said. "I had to try, but we knew right away it wasn't going to work. Why get hurt worse? There was nothing I could do, especially in a game that physical. I was trying to play with one arm."

Kentucky didn't mind knocking a few people to the floor. They weren't going down without a fight. May never returned.

"In all my years, that was the best college basketball I ever saw," Reed said. "It might have also been the most physical. It was a war out there, it really was. Kentucky was balanced and they had so much depth, they didn't care how many fouls they committed. They just pushed and shoved Indiana as much as they could and tried to make it very difficult for them. For May, it was just way too physical to be trying to play with one arm.

"That Kentucky team, they were on a mission. They took the approach that 'we might lose but we're not going to get pushed around. They did the pushing. They have fouls to give and they used them."

Kentucky also changed its approach on offense. And it worked to perfection.

"Coach Hall knew how good Indiana's half-court defense was so he just wanted us to come up and shoot as fast as we could," Kentucky's Mike Flynn said. "He turned me loose, and Jimmy Dan (Conner) and Kevin (Grevey) too. I loved it. I mean, you don't usually hear something like that from your coach, to just shoot away. I had my best college game that night, no doubt about it. I scored 22 and we played great against a really good team.

"We really wanted to teach Coach Knight a lesson that game. We really thought he was arrogant and had gotten too big for his britches. And we never forgot what he did to Coach Hall."

Kentucky had played zone against Indiana in December

and the Hoosiers shredded it. This time, they played aggressive man-to-man the entire time. When Indiana players would set screens in its motion offense, UK players didn't mind running right through them. Sometimes fouls were called, sometimes they weren't. Knight barked at the officials incessantly and the IU fans in Dayton never stopped screaming at the officials.

It was that physical.

But it was also that good.

It was tied 16-all when May left and UK led 24-18 a few minutes later. IU got hot behind Green and Benson to get up 38-31 but it was 44-all by halftime. Every possession on both ends of the court was an epic battle. Green got pushed to the ground once with no call made and picked up a technical foul when he complained. Knight got whistled for a technical later, as well.

IU went ahead 68-67 on a Buckner jumper with 8:54 left, but it would be their last lead of the game. Kentucky continued to push the pace and jumped out to a 10-point lead with four minutes left. Indiana kept scrapping. But every time they got close, things didn't go their way. There was a questionable illegal block call down the stretch, a head-shaking intentional foul for elbowing on Benson, an even more incredible technical foul on Green and even a couple of layups that hung on the rim and didn't go in.

Benson, who would finish with 33 points and 22 rebounds, had 12 down the stretch and a Laskowski free throw made it 90-88 with 30 seconds left. Kentucky got the ball across midcourt but Buckner and reserve Wayne Radford cornered Kevin Grevey in a trap. Hoping for a jump ball call, instead Buckner was called for a foul. Grevey made both free throws. Laskowski scored again with 14 seconds to go to make it 92-90 but IU couldn't get the ball back. They deflected one UK pass out of bounds after a timeout but then were forced to foul with just a few seconds to go. Jimmy Dan

Connor missed the free throw but time ran out before IU could do anything.

The dream was over. And it really hurt.

"I felt bad for the seniors, because it was their last shot," Buckner said about the loss. "We were so focused all year, always in tune, working every day minute by minute. But they certainly came into that game with plenty of incentive. We had embarrassed them earlier and they had some Indiana guys who really took it personally when they were playing us.

"We had what I thought was the best team. I never blamed it on Scott's injury. I actually thought he played pretty well when he was in there. Other guys stepped up all year. We just missed a lot of shots that day that we usually made."

The Hoosiers shot only 47 percent, far below their season average. They also had a season-high 20 turnovers, with the aggressive UK defense getting 10 steals, many of which led to easy baskets.

"Knight would never admit it at the time, but that was his most bitter loss," Reed said. "I think he panicked with May. The game was so fast and so physical that Scott really couldn't be effective with his arm the way it was. Even without him, they really, really battled. Benson was fantastic and Steve Green, he was just a great, great player, especially for that system."

Following the game, Knight explained the decision to start May … and the decision to go without him a few minutes later.

"We thought if they were playing a zone, we wanted our best shooters in there," Knight said after the game. "But it became a quickly paced game, and I just didn't feel Scott was able to catch the ball and move quickly enough."

Knight also gave Kentucky its props. After all, the Wildcats scored 92 points, the most IU had given up in Knight's first

67

four years. "I really feel in today's game the best team won," he said, "and that's sure as hell the way it ought to be."

Even the IU players noticed a different Kentucky team. They saw the fire in their eyes.

"They were ready for us right from the start. We had embarrassed them and they were really mad. They were ready to get back at us," Laskowski said. "Coach thought Scott was well enough to start and we were really confident going into that game. It was nice having Scott back, but even if he couldn't go we still thought we were good enough to beat them. Scott had that big bandage on his arm and it just didn't play out well. He had to come out after just a couple of minutes and I think that really fired up the Kentucky team, too.

"We just don't give up 92 points in a game. That's not us. But they were so jacked up and they just kept making shot after shot. Even without Scott we figured we could do it. But you have to give credit to them. They just had that mindset that they weren't going to let us beat them again, and for that one night they made it happen."

Clearly, though, it would have been a different story if May had been healthy. He was that good. A year later, May would be the consensus national player of the year when IU went 32-0 and won that elusive national championship. He was the second overall pick in the NBA draft following the season.

Buckner came back with May to enjoy the '76 season as well. He has a surprising take on the '75 loss.

"I haven't been haunted by it for one minute," Buckner said. "I have no regrets at all. They beat us. They played better and they deserved to win. When that next year rolled around it was different. Coach challenged us to win every game that year in '76. He knew we were capable. And we were."

Buckner has always been praised for being the leader of those great teams, but he takes the accolades with a grain of salt. It wasn't just him, he says.

"I've always appreciated all the kind words through the years about being a great leader and all, but to be honest it was a very easy team to lead. We had a lot of good players who worked hard and were very smart," Buckner said. "Coach Knight always had everyone well prepared and our self-confidence was very high. Plus, he pushed us hard and I think everyone wanted to make sure he was pleased with what you did. Everybody got it. Leading smart guys is easy, but they all challenged me every day, too. We had great camaraderie, and that was the bond Coach Knight created."

Knight certainly did wonderful things on the court with this IU team. They were exceptional, no question, and even in defeat they still came just a few points short of advancing past Kentucky. Had they gotten past the Wildcats, who knows what would have happened. With another week of healing, maybe May could have been more effective. Maybe.

UCLA beat Kentucky in the finals to win that 1975 title, with legendary coach John Wooden winning his 10th and final title before retiring. Kentucky came up short too, but their hurt wasn't as bad.

After all, they got their revenge against Indiana. That in itself outweighed the bitterness of losing to Wooden and UCLA in the final. Coach Joe B. Hall, who was on the verge of getting fired earlier in the year, was suddenly the acclaimed coach in Lexington.

"That win against Indiana in 1975 might have been the important win in school history for Kentucky," Reed said. "That turned it all around for Hall. He was never really criticized for losing to UCLA in the finals – at least not by the majority – and he turned right around and won the title in 1978 with a lot of those

**IU Archives P-0055947**

Senior John Laskowski (right) earned the nickname "Super Sub" for his role as IU's sixth man. He even made the cover of Sports Illustrated in '75.

freshmen who played quality minutes in that win against Indiana in '75.

"I mean, seriously, what happens if it does all fall apart after that Indiana loss back in December? It's a completely different season and a completely different future maybe, right? But after Knight insulted all of UK people with that slap to the head, everyone seemed to rally around that program. They considered it a very insulting gesture. On the court, the seniors took over and they turned their season around right after that. Under Rupp, Kentucky was the premier program and they had lost that. Suddenly they had it back, and that year it was at Indiana's expense.

"That, I'm sure, was very difficult for the IU fan base to swallow."

The spin after the game was that IU's season didn't end on March 22 with the loss to Kentucky, that it had ended a month earlier when May broke his arm at Purdue on Feb. 22.

But the 31 straight wins notwithstanding, the prelude for the heartbreaking season-ending loss might go back further, to that day in early December when Indiana embarrassed Kentucky on the floor but then Knight slapped Hall in the head and changed the entire dynamic of the day.

He made it personal for those Kentucky players – very personal – and when they got their shot at revenge, they took it. They outplayed the Hoosiers in the NCAA tournament and extracted their pound of flesh.

"We respected each other as players and we didn't have any animosity toward the Indiana players, just the coach. We hated Coach Knight and hated what he did to our coach," Flynn said. "But it meant so much to us that day to beat a really great team. Maybe if they had May it would have been different, but maybe not. We played great that day. That was our day, finally.

"I was the last one to cut down the net, and I was shaking it at all those IU fans. I've still got people mad at me about that. But it just felt so good to beat them. There was no doubt it was personal for me, for all of us."

IU fans have bristled for years that a broken arm cost us that 1975 banner, but an unnecessary slap to the head played a big role, too.

That can't ever be forgotten.

**PhotoShop Created Image**

The 2013 Indiana Hoosiers were ranked No. 1 in the preseason and won the Big Ten regular season title in dramatic fashion.

# Chapter 5

**Just a few weeks after** Kentucky had ended Indiana's 2011-12 season with a 102-90 victory in the Sweet Sixteen in Atlanta – yes, Kentucky again – the college basketball media began to look ahead to the 2012-13 season.

And most everyone was arriving at the same conclusion: Indiana was going to be loaded.

ESPN.com was the first to predict that Indiana would be the No. 1 team in the nation when the preseason polls were revealed prior to the 2012-13 season. USA Today, Yahoo Sports and The Sporting News were quick to follow suit. When the "official poll" – the Associated Press Top 25 – came out with its preseason poll, IU was indeed the No. 1 team in the land.

And it should have been.

Indiana, only five years removed from the dumpster fire that was the Kelvin Sampson era, was getting the country's stamp of approval as the best team in America. It had all the pieces in place to make a run at that elusive sixth NCAA championship banner. There had been a few Indiana teams since Steve Alford, Keith Smart and company won it all in 1987 that had made IU fans believe that a sixth national title was more than a dream, but this was clearly one of them.

Indiana was returning all five starters and some key subs from a team that spent the final 14 weeks of the previous season ranked in the top 25.

IU's top five scorers returned and those five had accounted for an average of 59.3 points and 23.3 rebounds all by themselves.

75

Other returnees accounted for another 9 points per game. That was more than 68 points off of a team that averaged 77.3 the year before.

The focal point was sophomore Cody Zeller, who had started all 36 games his freshman season and led the Hoosiers in scoring and rebounding with averages of 15.6 points and 6.6 rebounds. He had been tabbed the Big Ten's Freshman of the Year in his first season at IU and was the preseason national player of the year by The Sporting News when it announced that team prior to the start of Zeller's sophomore season.

Christian Watford was back at one forward spot after averaging 12.6 points per game the year before and hitting one of the biggest shots in program history that beat No. 1 Kentucky at Assembly Hall. Watford also averaged 5.8 rebounds as a junior and hit nearly 44 percent of his shots from beyond the 3-point arc. He was a big body with good outside range that forced opposing teams to account for him.

Indiana also had two returning starting guards in Jordan Hulls, a former Indiana Mr. Basketball from Bloomington South, who averaged 11.7 points per game as a junior and was a deadeye shooter. Hulls hit 50.4 percent from the field as a junior and 49 percent from 3-point range. He also almost never missed at the free throw line, where he was a 90 percent foul shooter.

Victor Oladipo had started 34 games the year before and averaged 10.8 points per game along with 5.3 rebounds. He was one of IU's most athletic players that simply seemed to get better with each passing game. His weakness coming into his junior season was his perimeter shooting, hitting only 20.8 percent from beyond the arc as a sophomore. But after spending countless hours in the gym the summer prior to his junior season, that was about to change in a big way.

Will Sheehey was the other player who had started 11 games the year before and had averaged 8.6 points per game. It was his shot from the baseline that had proved to be the game-winner in the NCAA Tournament victory over VCU in Portland, Ore.

Sheehey would become one of the best sixth-men in the country because there was no room in the starting lineup for him.

The fifth spot was going to a freshman. A freshman who had been on the radar of Hoosier fans since he was in a fifth grade.

Yogi Ferrell, finally, had made his way to Bloomington. "The Movement" had begun.

\*\*\*   \*\*\*   \*\*\*

**It was ironic that** IU was No. 1 in the nation *and* had a great recruiting class, one that would turn Indiana basketball back into an elite program once again.

The jewel in that recruiting class was Kevin 'Yogi' Ferrell, the McDonald's All-American from Park Tudor High School in Indianapolis. Ferrell had led his team to the state championship game his last three seasons, winning titles as both a junior and a senior. He appeared to a missing piece for IU coach Tom Crean because he would become the facilitator in the Indiana offense as the point guard.

There were other solid players in that class who got rave reviews. Hanner Mosquera-Perea was a 6-foot-8 power forward who had a long wingspan and appeared to be very athletic. Jeremy Hollowell, also 6-8, had a nice outside shot and looked to be a player who would challenge for minutes. Peter Jurkin was a 7-footer that looked to be a project but appeared at first to have more immediate potential than recent big projects like Tijan Jobe and Bawa Muniru that had passed quickly through the program.

A fifth player in the class was Ron Patterson, a shooting guard from Indianapolis Broad Ripple, who ultimately was an academic casualty and never played at IU. But no one knew that yet. Instead, the IU Nation looked at the incoming class mixed with the returning players and believed it was about to see something special. Ferrell, Hollowell and Patterson were all Indiana All-Stars and IU fans have always been big on keeping the best talent within the state.

The freshmen were a nice addition, but IU also got a huge boost from not losing anybody. After 2012, both Zeller and Watford could have turned pro and no one would have batted an eye. Zeller, even after one year, was NBA ready. Watford had a huge, high-profile junior year and certainly could have earned a paycheck somewhere.

In the end, however, both players decided to stay in Bloomington and that hype just increased.

"I came back for one reason, and that was because I believed we had the pieces in place to win a national championship," Watford said. "We had been talking about that since we stepped on campus in Bloomington as freshman. We had truly believed that we could be the group that turned things around and could do it. No one believed us at the time because IU basketball was going through a tough time, but by the time we had arrived at our senior year, there was a feeling like we could really do it."

IU coach Tom Crean said he thought having Watford back was a piece in the puzzle that Indiana really needed.

"Christian really ended the season on a high note on the biggest stage and is building off that," Crean said the day that Watford opted to return to school for his senior year. "He is going to have the opportunity to be a leader and have an even greater impact on the program and his game. But more importantly, he will earn his degree from IU."

Zeller was certain the NBA would be there for him when he was ready and he just felt like there was some unfinished business at IU.

"I grew up hoping that one day I would get the opportunity to play in the NBA, but at this point, I'm not ready for my college experience to be over," Zeller said the day he decided to return. "Coach Crean and my family were very supportive and helpful as I made my decision. My college experience at IU this year has exceeded my expectations, on and off the court. I look forward to playing at Assembly Hall next year in front of the greatest fans in the country."

So just how good was the group that IU had assembled to return for the 2012-13 season?

Consider this: At Indiana there's an elite club made up of players who scored more than 1,000 points in their careers. Calbert Cheaney tops that list as the all-time leading scorer in IU and Big Ten history with 2,613 points. A total of five players have eclipsed the 2,000-point mark with Steve Alford, Don Schlundt, A.J. Guyton and Mike Woodson being the others.

In more than 110 years of Indiana basketball history, less than 50 players have ever scored more than 1,000 points in their IU careers.

And this team had five who would ultimately be able to claim that honor.

Four would play on the court at the same time having each scored more than 1,000 points for their careers, including Hulls, Oladipo, Watford and Zeller. If you could have gazed into a crystal ball back then, you would have known that the other starter on that team, freshman point guard Yogi Ferrell, would go on to do the same in his IU career, too.

**Mike Dickbernd/IU Athletics**
Tom Crean inherited a mess when he came to Indiana, but by the time the 2012-13 season rolled around, he had IU ranked No. 1 in the land.

Ken Bikoff, longtime IU beat writer for both Inside Indiana and Peegs.com, said it was an IU basketball team that truly had it all.

"Watford and Hulls had been through hell and back to build the program, and both knew their roles well," Bikoff said. "Cody was a special college player, someone who could have been even more effective if he had been allowed to stretch his legs a little from the perimeter. The kid had a nice jumper. But he was so effective inside and in so many ways – passing out of the double team, driving, rebounding, scoring with his back to the basket, defending in short spaces – that few teams could match him. And Victor was just blossoming with each passing game. It will be a long time before I see another player who just gained more and more confidence every time he was on the court. Yogi was smart enough to avoid trying to do too much on the floor. He was effective enough to give opponents headaches, and he was young enough to not realize when the pressure was really on.

"You had size, quickness, experience, shooting, passing, a game-changing defender. It was a lineup without a real weakness save for a lack of size in the backcourt."

Jake Query, the Indianapolis radio talk show host with WNDE 1260-AM, said the 2013 IU team had the most talent a Tom Crean-coached team has ever had.

"He had four 1,000-point scorers (at that time), a McDonalds All-American point guard, a 7-footer, the perfect mix of leadership/seniors with emerging and developing talent, two lottery picks, and a sixth man of the year," Query said. "Not really sure what else you would want."

Don Fischer, the play-by-play voice of Indiana basketball, said there was no question about how much talent that team had, but for him it was even more than that.

"What I liked about that team more than anything else was that there was a basketball IQ," Fischer said. "To me that team would compare with most of the great teams in Indiana history from a basketball IQ standpoint. They were smart, they understood the game, they understood how to play together and they believed in themselves. I think a big part of being successful is believing that you're good and believing that you can win every game and I think that team had that going for them."

IU fans were certainly getting excited. Demand for student season tickets was at an all-time high. Indiana already boasted the largest student section in the nation, with 7,800 of the 17,000-and-change seats at Assembly Hall set aside for the kids.

By mid-summer, IU had already sold 10,000 student season tickets for the 2012-13 season and announced it would cap that number had 12,400, which would allow students to get to see a minimum of 10 of the 16 home games in the upcoming season. Well before the season began, that 12,400 number was reached as well. Excitement on campus was heating up as well.

Now the Hoosiers simply had to live up to all of the hype.

*** *** ***

**E**ntering the offseason, Indiana coach Tom Crean talked about the things he believed the Hoosiers needed to do to position themselves for a solid run. He said that individual improvement went without saying, but he felt that IU needed to improve in three areas to really put things all together: strength, winning individual battles and playing better defense.

Crean said adding strength was Job One.

"When we measure ourselves against the best players and the best teams, there were times when we weren't strong enough,

82

whether it was just maturity-wise in body or whether it was age or whether it was just plain will power," Crean said. "Whatever it was, we've got to be stronger in more situations. We've got to have more thickness to us. We've got to have more stability in that strength game."

Winning those individual battles was also something that Crean was adamant about in the offseason.

"We've got to win more one-on-one type of battles whether it is a 50-50 ball, whether it's stopping somebody one-on-one, whether it's the ability to break somebody down, not be better one-on-one players but win more one-on-one situations and there is a difference," Crean said. "Because our ability to share the ball this year, our ability to move the ball, our ability to play through and at Cody (Zeller) and have so many people do so many good things and so many people jump in numbers, it can really take another step if we can get better in those individual match-ups. We can get better in those individual situations and that's what this time of year is for."

Defense was also on Crean's mind. He had just seen his team give up 102 points in the Sweet Sixteen loss to Kentucky. That was unacceptable.

"If we're better defensively, we'll be a better defensive rebounding team, we'll be able to play at a faster pace because our defense will allow so many things to happen for us," Crean said. "We'll be able to get out in transition that much more. We'll be able to create off turnovers that much more and they all go hand-and-hand, especially the strength and the defense."

If Watford could have added a fourth, he would have said accountability.

"I expected our team to pretty much pick up where we had left off the year before in a lot of ways and at the same time get used to all of the new moving parts we had coming in," Watford said when interviewed in the spring of 2015. "But the most important that we could do going into that season was to hold each other accountable and hold each other to a higher standard. And I really felt like, as that season progressed, that we were able to do just that."

Crean was asked at the time if he believed that the summer of 2012 was any more important than other seasons in terms of building up a veteran team.

"They're all important," Crean said. "It was as important to me and our coaching staff the first couple summers. Maybe the players didn't understand what that was all about, they probably didn't. Last year it really, really started to take shape. We've always had players that worked pretty hard. But there have always been guys where they aren't spending the time at it that they

**Mike Dickbernd/IU Athletics**
Will Sheehey played an important role off the bench for Indiana and played key minutes down the stretch of games. He was a huge fan favorite as well thanks to his high energy level and engaging smile.

needed to spend. Those days are over. You can't function here if you don't have that kind of mentality anymore."

Crean knew what he had with this team, and he knew what he wanted.

The players knew what they wanted to.

***     ***     ***

**J**ordan Hulls could feel it as the 2013 season approached. The local hero from Bloomington could already feel the expectations. And that was just fine with him.

"There aren't too many players or teams that can go into offseason workouts with the notion that they have a legitimate chance of winning a national championship, and yet we were one of the few," Hulls said. "We had all the pieces. We had great shooting, could play inside and out, solid bench, defense, and most importantly, we had heart. We had a team full of guys with chips on their shoulder."

That chip had been a result of all of the bad things that had happened to the Indiana basketball program since Kelvin Sampson brought the program to its knees because of NCAA rules violations following the 2008 season. Two years after IU had hit the lowest of lows, players like Hulls, Watford and Maurice Creek had been instrumental in turning the program around. Guys like Will Sheehey and Oladipo would come next and eventually Zeller. Then "The Movement," led by Ferrell, arrived when Hulls, Watford and Derek Elston were seniors.

The year before Hulls and his class arrived at IU, the Hoosiers had suffered through a dismal 6-25 campaign that included a 1-17 Big Ten record in Crean's first season with the Hoosiers. Crean had to blow up the program to go forward and he cleaned house of all the trouble-makers.

IU had two players that returned from the year before in Kyle Taber and walk-on Brett Finkelmeier. Crean filled the roster full of players that likely wouldn't have been playing Big Ten basketball under most circumstances.

When Hulls' class arrived, IU took a step forward by going 10-21 and 4-14 in conference the next season. As sophomores, with Sheehey and Oladipo now on board, IU would improve to 12-20 but still just 3-15 in conference play. It took the addition of a player like Zeller the following year to really get IU headed in the right direction. That team, in Hulls' junior season, would go 27-9 and knock off No. 1 Kentucky along the way on Christian Watford's three-pointer – "Watford for the win!" that was replayed over and over on ESPN for the rest of that season.

All that agony had given way to this, a No. 1 preseason ranking. Thousands of hours of hard work was paying off.

"We had dealt with being on the very bottom and had to fight and claw our way for everything," Hulls said. "Going through those tough experiences, the juniors and seniors, it built the foundation for our work ethic, determination, and mindset that was needed to be the best. We were able to then pass those traits down to the underclassmen, who were really good already but learned quickly what exactly it took to play at the level and standards we had set for ourselves.

"We understood that it doesn't matter who gets the credit or scores the most points. As long as we play together and win, that's all that mattered."

Hulls said that particular team had a special bond.

"Our group was special and we knew it," Hulls said. "Being close off the court also was key in our success. We could all hang out and have fun together and I really think that carried over to the court. Of course, we had our scuffles in practices but that's what separated us, too. We all were competitors and hated to lose."

Derek Elston was a 6-foot-9 senior forward from Tipton (Ind.) when the 2012-13 season arrived. He also knew how special that team camaraderie was. When you have a group of players that genuinely like each other, it just makes everything that much easier, he said.

"To the fans, we were pieces to their puzzle, but for us we were all great friends with one goal to accomplish," Elston said. "I've seen teams that have had some unreal individual players that can't achieve anything special because their ego is put before the team. But we never had that ... ever."

Elston said what that group did best was come together under Crean's leadership and focus on the important things.

"We had Vic and Cody and Christian, those guys had every right to say 'Get me the ball and get out of my way.' but as soon as Coach Crean saw any sign of that, whether it be in practice or a game, we were all punished for it," Elston said. "Basketball isn't supposed to be fun. You have to work to exhaustion to achieve a goal. Winning is fun, and when you can enjoy the group of guys who you are winning with, that makes it worth everything."

The 2011-12 season had signaled the beginning of change for an Indiana basketball team that had fallen on difficult times. The 2012-13 team, however, would have a different challenge ahead of it. Teams in recent seasons had been able to get away with playing the underdog card. Those days were over.

Crean said it was all about how you defined it.

"The perception on the outside isn't necessarily the perception on the inside," Crean said in the spring of 2012. "The guys that I've been around in those workouts and the guys that have been in the weight room the last three weeks, I don't have concerns

87

about how hungry they're going to be. That's even before we're all together in the summertime. Those things are fun to talk about and they're interesting, but when you're in-house, and you're inside of it every day, if someone was acting like that, I think it would show up pretty quick. I haven't seen any of that and, if the day comes, I think it will be short-lived."

For the players that had been through all the pain and suffering that IU had endured in previous years, all the hype that came with Indiana's No. 1 ranking headed into the 2012-13 season was simply the way they believed the story deserved to be written.

For the newcomers, though, it was a little different. They had watched the carnage that was IU basketball after the Sampson mess and they had seen Crean slowly put the program back together.

When Ferrell first set foot on the Bloomington campus, he truly believed he was about to be a part of something very special in the upcoming season at Indiana. And he was ready.

"We had a really nice starting five with every piece," Ferrell said during a 2015 interview prior to his senior year at IU. "And we were just loaded with experience. The only place where we didn't have experience was my position, and I felt supremely confident, especially lining up with that kind of talent around me.

"I think all of us truly believed that the sky was the limit for our team and that we were on the brink of doing something incredible."

On the brink. They certainly were.

# Chapter 6

When the 2012-13 season finally arrived, the Hoosiers were tired of hearing about how good they were supposed to be. It was time to show it. IU was the No. 1-ranked team in the nation and that target was firmly affixed to its backs.

Indiana opened at home against Bryant and won easily, 97-54. The most memorable moment from that night came before tipoff when IU athletic director Fred Glass announced to a capacity crowd at Assembly Hall that he had given Tom Crean a contract extension through the 2020 season as a way of showing his appreciation for how Crean had successfully brought Indiana basketball back.

"Tom Crean has done an absolutely phenomenal job bringing Indiana University back to its rightful place as one of the elite basketball programs in the country," Glass said that evening. "His energy, integrity, ability, passion, industry, vision, and commitment are unparalleled"

Next, IU played a couple of early cupcakes in North Dakota State and Sam Houston State and had predictable outcomes. IU won the first game by 26 points and the second by 54. Indiana would win its first nine games of the season and seven of them were by 24 points or more.

All patsies? Not at all. One of those wins was very, very special to everyone in Hoosier Nation. Fans, players and coaches included.

*** *** ***

Indiana drew legendary North Carolina in the ACC/Big Ten Challenge and when the game finally rolled around, Assembly Hall was at a fever pitch. Everyone had been waiting for this game for months, and it showed.

And they loved every minute of it when the Hoosiers pounded the No. 13-ranked but obviously overmatched Tar Heels 83-59.

Cody Zeller had 20 points on 8 of 13 shooting and consistently ran the floor and beat the Tar Heels back to the other end for easy baskets. Will Sheehey played 26 minutes off the bench and scored 19, hitting 8 of 12 shots.

Yogi Ferrell considered that game one of his highlights of his freshman season. Before enrolling a IU, Ferrell had been in Assembly Hall a few times for games when the crowd had been really loud. But he had never played in a game where the level of intensity with the crowd was completely bonkers like it was that night.

"That was probably the loudest game I had ever attended, played in or been a part of," Ferrell said. "I was riled up, basically. The fans were so crazy and we were up by 20 and just killing them. Everything was working right. That was probably one of the most fun games I've played in in my career."

Jordan Hulls echoed Ferrell's sentiments.

"North Carolina was a very talented, highly ranked team and we just absolutely destroyed them in front of the best fans in the country," Hulls said.

Ken Bikoff, longtime IU beat writer for both Inside Indiana and Peegs.com, also was impressed.

"The first half they played against North Carolina that year was the best 20 minutes of basketball I've ever seen an Indi-

90

ana team play in my life," Bikoff said. "They were crisp, they were confident and they were dominant even though it was only a nine-point lead at the break."

Cody Zeller said he was proud of the mentality his team took against a program like North Carolina. Zeller knew North Carolina well because his older brother Tyler and played there and UNC was in his final three – along with Butler – before he picked Indiana in the important recruiting battle.

"We had to be the hunters, not the hunted," Zeller said in the postgame interview that night. "We can't be comfortable with where we are at. We've got to keep every game like we're the underdog and keep attacking and we'll get better."

Crean gushed about his team in his postgame remarks and tried to downplay the significance of beating a program like North Carolina by that many points at Assembly Hall.

"I haven't thought about that much," Crean said. "You get so caught up in the moment. Our team just keeps getting better, and I think the key is that we don't get away from that. There's got to be humbleness, there's got to be a confidence, but at the same time, you're building your edge constantly, daily. We can't get away from that. I don't spend a lot of time thinking that way, and I don't think we will."

Derek Elston had a different memory of that game. He said it didn't take long for this IU team to realize that the season had a chance to be a memorable one and the North Carolina game certainly reinforced that. But Elston remembered the film session the next day, too.

"The scary thing was, we were still criticized in the film room that next day," Elston recalled. "Coach (Crean) kept saying we could play so much better, and we knew it."

In his postgame remarks, North Carolina coach Roy Williams praised the level at which Indiana had been able to play the game.

"I have to congratulate Indiana, and boy I would have loved to watch them play if it wasn't against my team," Williams said. "You look down the lineup and Cody Zeller is really a load to handle and two other guys that I didn't even hear of while they were in high school just kicked our rear ends. You look at Hulls and think, 'That's really something – 5 of 8 (shooting), eight assists, and zero turnovers.' Yogi was six assists and one turnover.

"But Oladipo, man what an aggressive basketball player

**Mike Dickbernd/IU Athletics**
Indiana's Jordan Hulls fends off a defender during a game at Assembly Hall in the 2013 season.

he is. The stat sheet says he had one block and zero steals, but I felt like he stole the ball from us 10 times. His energy level for them on the offensive and defensive ends of the floor was really something."

Really something, indeed. It was a special night for Indiana basketball.

*** *** ***

**The other two good** wins in that run were earlier against Georgia and Georgetown in the Progressive Legends Classic at the Barclays Center in Bloomington.

IU beat Georgia 66-53 in the first game – a game where former IU coach Bob Knight was the color commentator for ESPN, by the way – and then later beat a good Georgetown team 82-72 in the tournament title game. That Georgetown team would go on to be considered for a No. 1 NCAA Tournament seed later in March.

Hulls said the win over Georgetown was big for IU's credibility at that point in the season carrying the lofty No. 1 ranking.

"That was our first test on a big stage as the No. 1 team in the country, playing against Georgia and then Georgetown," Hulls said. "For me, it was one of my favorite individual accomplishments of that season. I would say that winning MVP of the Legends Classic Tournament was a great accomplishment for me. I couldn't have done it without my teammates obviously, but I was fortunate to have a great start to our season by playing well and, most importantly, impact winning."

Hulls had 14 against Georgia including 4 of 6 three-pointers and then had a game-high 17 points and three more triples against Georgetown.

IU's lone blemish in the nonconference season was a tough

93

pill to swallow as the Hoosiers lost to Butler 88-86 in overtime in the Crossroads Classic at Bankers Life Fieldhouse in Indianapolis. Butler guard Alex Barlow's spinning 6-footer with 2.4 seconds to play in overtime proved to be the winner. IU then beat three inferior opponents to take a 12-1 record into the Big Ten season.

"Losing to Butler really hurt because it was Butler," IU senior forward Christian Watford said. "And I'm not taking anything away from Butler, but it was just more that it was an in-state rival and that was just one thing we didn't want to do. I wasn't even from Indiana and I knew how important it was for a program like IU to always beat the state schools."

About the only red flag during the early part of the season was a lack of depth on the front line. Derek Elston missed the first 10 games of the season after undergoing knee surgery. Compounding the problem, two of the promising freshmen, Hanner Mosquera-Perea and Peter Jurkin, were ruled ineligible for nine games by the NCAA for receiving impermissible benefits from their AAU coach while still in high school.

In early December, IU lost another forward – this one for the season – when reserve Austin Etherington fractured the patella in his left leg during a 100-69 victory over Central Connecticut State. IU wasn't taking hits to its top six or seven players, but the hits were still coming nonetheless.

Still, it was good to be through the nonconference season. The Hoosiers had played well, mostly. But it was just a start.

***   ***   ***

**The Hoosiers won their** first three in Big Ten play, including two wins on the road at Iowa and Penn State before coming home to beat No. 8 Minnesota at home, 88-81. All of a sudden

IU was 15-1. The loss to Bulter had cost the Hoosiers their No. 1 ranking, falling to No. 6. By the time it beat Minnesota at home, Indiana was back up to No. 2 in the country.

Hulls remembered the Iowa game for all the wrong reasons. Yes, he was happy to go on the road to open Big Ten play and get a 69-65 victory over a Hawkeye team that was 11-2 in non-conference play. But he was frustrated with his own performance. Hulls couldn't hit anything. He started and played 22 minutes but didn't score. He missed all 10 of his shots from the field, including four 3-pointers. Luckily for Hulls, IU had a pair of double-double performances from Zeller and Oladipo. Zeller had 19 points and 10 rebounds and Oladipo had 14 points and 10 rebounds.

"I was disappointed but at the same time I felt good about the fact that we had a team where if someone had an off game, someone else would be there to pick them up," Hulls said. "That was the kind of team we had. We had a lot of players who could really hurt you."

The 3-0 start was short-lived because next up for the Hoosiers was a 12-4 Wisconsin team that would give IU fits. The Badgers had been one team that IU hadn't been able to beat for a long time. In fact, going into that gam,e which was the only meeting of the season between the two teams, the Badgers had won 10 in a row. Make it 11 as Wisconsin posted a 64-59 victory that again dropped IU to No. 7 in the nation.

Hulls had another tough game shooting the ball and that, coupled with losing to Wisconsin again, was a difficult pill to swallow. This time he was 2-of-8 from the field and finished with four points in 32 minutes.

"I just remember not playing so well and missing shots," Hulls said. "I always hate it when I miss a lot of shots because I hold myself to a high standard and am a perfectionist, so when I don't see results I get frustrated. Also, we had never beat Wisconsin in my four years, so it made it extra tough."

The next five games, however, were all wins, including home victories against two more ranked opponents. IU beat No. 13 Michigan State 75-70 on Jan. 26, and then after a 37-point road win at Purdue, the Hoosiers came home to face No. 1 Michigan in a nationally televised game on ESPN that also featured an appearance from the ESPN GameDay crew.

Michigan came into the game with a 20-1 record overall and tied for first with IU with 7-1 conference marks.

IU didn't disappoint in that one. Zeller had 19 points and 10 rebounds and Watford also had a double-double with 14 points and 10 rebounds as IU posted an 81-73 win and reached the halfway point in the Big Ten season with an 8-1 Big Ten record.

The Hoosiers would also regain the No. 1 spot in the nation for the next four weeks.

No. 1, but with a question mark.

*** *** ***

The big question that would be asked with this Indiana basketball team, however, is whether the Hoosiers peaked too soon. On Feb. 2, after IU had beat Michigan in the bright lights of national television, the Hoosiers were 20-2 and clearly looked the part of a team that could win the national championship.

Over the final 14 games of the season, however, IU would go 9-5.

"Unfortunately, in some ways I think we did peak a little early," Watford said. "We just played so well that year up until about that Michigan game but after that it just seemed like things were a little different."

Ken Bikoff, the longtime IU beat writer for both Inside Indiana and Peegs.com, said there was no question in his mind that the team got tired in the second half of the season.

"They did look different down the stretch," Bikoff said. "They got tired. I don't think there's any question about that. Cody wasn't as explosive as he was earlier in the season or during his freshman year. The pressure of being No. 1 was heavy that year. Everyone on the team seemed to feel it. And remember, IU had a number of weeks in which it lost, but it remained at No. 1 because the Nos. 2, 3 and 4 in the country lost, as well. They also had dropped to No. 6 or No. 7 in the rankings a couple of times, and I think the team felt the weight of expectations."

Bikoff believes that no one felt the pressure more, however, than IU head coach Tom Crean.

"I've talked to Crean about this myself," Bikoff said. "I told him that he was a piano wire for that entire season, tighter than he had ever been before or since. He was just different when that team was No. 1. He felt the pressure, and I think the team felt it, too. When they started to stumble, everyone tightened up even more, and it left everyone that much more fatigued mentally as much as physically."

Dave Furst, the sports anchor at WRTV-Channel 6 in Indianapolis, remembers thinking that team was gassed, too.

"The numbers don't lie," Furst said. "Too bad the NCAA tourney wasn't played in February."

Greg Rakestraw, the longtime radio man in the Indianapolis market, said the problem was that injuries at fatigue had reduced the IU team to one of very few options.

"I think that team had clearly played its best basketball earlier in the season," Rakestraw said. "Players like (Jeremy) Hollowell and (Hanner) Mosquera-Perea never had the impact even in limited minutes as freshmen that Tom Crean thought they would. And due to injuries, (Derek) Elston didn't have much left to give that group. You felt like Will Sheehey was a sixth starter but after that, it was (Remy) Abell and that was about it."

That lack of depth would start to show.

*** *** ***

The next game, at Illinois, was one that left the Hoosiers with a bad feeling in their stomachs and left a crowd at the other Assembly Hall in Champaign, Ill. storming the court in celebration.

This one was basically gift-wrapped for the Illini. IU had a 14-point lead with two minutes to play in the first half and the Hoosiers looked to have the game under control with a 10-point lead with five minutes to play in the game. Illinois rallied though, and the game was tied with 0.9 seconds to play and the ball out of bounds under the Illini basket.

Somehow, Illinois senior Tyler Griffey broke free on the inbounds play and scored a layup at the buzzer to give the Illini a 74-72 win. The 8-1 Hoosiers had just gotten beat by the 2-7 Illini.

Yogi Ferrell still shakes his head when he thinks about that one. He said it was a complete lack of communication on that final play and held himself responsible.

"That game was definitely a low point in that season," Ferrell said when looking back a few years later. "That was just a nail-biter and it was awful communication on me and Christian's part. It was kind of a broken play. People were just running around and setting screens and he just got a wide open layup.

"It was embarrassing."

Elston remembered two things about that game: One was how upset Crean was with their late-game performance and the

98

other was how everyone just assumed that loss would knock IU from its No. 1 perch.

"When we got beat at the buzzer, Coach was furious but he needed to be," Elston said. "We knew we messed that up, miscommunication led to that loss, and communication on the court is something we thought we excelled in, so that one did hurt.

"But when we woke up the next day we all thought it was pretty amusing that losing to our big arch-rival Illinois hadn't changed our perception nationally. That loss really meant nothing in the grand scheme, because we stayed the No. 1 team."

*** *** ***

**I**ndiana won the next four in a row, including big road wins at Michigan State and Ohio State. IU beat Purdue at home by 28, meaning that the Hoosiers had defeated their in-state rivals by 65 points in two games. Sheehey had 22 points in that game and hit all nine of his shots from the field.

The Michigan State game was huge because the Spartans had defeated IU 17 times in a row at the Breslin Center. It had been more than 20 years since IU had last won there in 1991.

"Winning at Michigan State at their place was special because an IU team hadn't done it in a long time, and it's never easy to win there," Hulls said. "You always enjoy the wins a little bit more when you're doing something that has been done in a long, long time."

A road loss at Minnesota and a home victory over Iowa set the Hoosiers up with a 13-3 record in conference play and at least share of the Big Ten title with two games to go.

It was two of the craziness nights in recent basketball memory at Indiana.

*** *** ***

The first game was Ohio State in Assembly Hall for Senior Night. Senior Night is an emotional game for IU and in this case it was even be more so because it would be the final game for Jordan Hulls, Christian Watford and Derek Elston, and ultimately for Cody Zeller and Victor Oladipo, who would declare for the NBA Draft.

Most IU fans expected the Hoosiers to win the conference title outright against an Ohio State team it had beaten 81-68 in Columbus less than a month before. And it was important that IU win, too. If the Hoosiers didn't win the title outright it would be considerably more difficult to do so against a top-10 Michigan team on the road in the conference finale.

**Mike Dickbernd/IU Athletics**
Christian Watford made a ton of big shots for Indiana during his brilliant four-year career. His name and "The Shot" against Kentucky are historic.

No one ever accused Indiana of doing things the easy way. Ohio State came in and knocked off IU 67-58 in a 9 p.m. weeknight game at Assembly Hall that took strange to a new level. The Senior Night speeches went on until well after midnight, and coaches and players didn't reach the media room at Assembly Hall until almost 1 a.m. Part of the reason for that was that Crean had his team cut down the nets following the game because it had officially clinched a share the Big Ten title. Still, many IU fans were disappointed with a decision to cut down the nets following a loss.

Dave Furst, sports anchor for WRTV Channel 6 in Indianapolis, said it took him a moment to really digest what was happening as he saw the players cutting down the nets after a loss.

"The team lost to Ohio State but they were cutting down nets?" Furst said. "I remember tweeting pictures as it happened, thinking the IU and Crean bashers will crucify the program for this one. And they did. But, you had to look at the big picture. I felt it was not just a celebration of a Big Ten championship, but a cleansing of the hell this program had gone through the years following the Kelvin Sampson debacle. I'm not sure fans, or even some media, truly understand how his hubris towards the NCAA and its rules took down such a tradition-rich program. But, Crean, his staff, and the players that night all knew."

So Furst was in the camp that gave IU a pass for the cutting down of the nets. Some weren't nearly as kind.

Longtime Indianapolis radio personality Greg Rakestraw called the whole thing embarrassing.

"I thought it cheapened the accomplishments of that group, not just of that season, but of their run in Bloomington," Rakestraw said. "There was no need for a participation trophy-event for those guys. They brought back Indiana basketball. It was like Tom had in his mind that they had to have that ceremony as a reward or thank you. If you wanted to cut down the nets, do it after the Michigan game once you get back to Bloomington. You could have announced it on social media, people would have shown up to watch it. That was embarrassing, and that's putting it nicely."

Some feel even more strongly that it was a moment that should have – at the very least – been delayed.

Pete DiPrimio, the longtime Indiana beat writer for the Fort Wayne News-Sentinel, called it a fiasco.

"It was not the right thing to do," DiPrimio said. "No one was in the mood to celebrate anything after the Ohio State loss. It should have been held at another time. IU should have had a separate ceremony for it. That was especially true given the Ohio State game had a 9 p.m. tipoff and you already had the Senior Night speeches to wait on. The whole fiasco irritated an already edgy fan base and generated a lot of media ill-will, especially from the national media, that IU didn't need."

Ken Bikoff, a longtime IU beat writer, said cutting down the nets was one of the weirdest moments in his career as a sports journalist.

"And it was one of the worst decisions of Tom Crean's time at IU," Bikoff said. "It should have never happened. Someone should have stepped in to stop that whole situation. It was an embarrassment for IU then, and it continues to be a sore spot for a lot of people."

Crean's explanation later was simply that IU's players had earned that moment.

"There was no question we were going to do that," Crean said. "These guys earned that. I have a responsibility to them. We're going to hang our own banner up there, and eventually we're going to individualize them. Guys have worked to the point where they have earned it. They've come in here and looked at those banners every day and now they're going to get a chance to hang one. Once Sunday came, that was a given."

Hulls said the final two games of the Big Ten season would turn out to be his lowest and then his highest moments of the entire season. Losing to Ohio State on Senior Night was obviously the lowest of lows.

"It really requires little explanation on why it's so upsetting, but it was the lowest point in my mind during the regular season," Hulls said. "We had a chance to win the Big Ten outright in front of our fans and it was the last game I would ever play in Assembly Hall. We didn't play well at all and it was embarrassing and sad because we wanted to win in front of our fans on that special night.

"And I hate losing."

$$*** \quad *** \quad ***$$

**As for the season** finale against the Wolverines in Ann Arbor, Mich., well, the rest, as they say, is history. Much like the Illinois game where the Hoosiers had squandered a big lead only to lose at the end, this time Indiana turned the script around in the season finale at Michigan.

The Wolverines needed a win to get a share of the Big Ten title and Michigan led by five points with under a minute to play before the Hoosiers scored the game's final six points to win. Zeller scored on a layup with 13 seconds to play to put the Hoosiers up 72-71 and then altered a shot by Trey Burke on the other end to seal the IU victory. Zeller finished with 25 points and 10 rebounds and Oladipo had 14 points and 13 rebounds.

Had Michigan won, IU would have finished in a four-way tie for first with Michigan, Michigan State and Ohio State. Instead,

IU won its first outright Big Ten title since 1993 and clinched the No. 1 seed in the Big Ten Tournament.

Hulls said the game ranks as his favorite moment from that season.

"We had just lost to Ohio State on Senior Night and knew that in order for us to win the Big Ten outright, we had to win on the road at Michigan," Hulls said. "They were a very good team, especially at their place, and it was the ultimate test for us. We had already clinched a share of the Big Ten title, but we weren't going to settle for that. The way we won that game, being down five points with 55 seconds left, resembled exactly what our team was all about, never giving up.

"We worked so hard to get to that point for ourselves and for Indiana Basketball, so to win it in that fashion was something I will never forget."

*** *** ***

**I**ndiana went into the Big Ten Tournament as the No. 1 seed and had an easy time with Illinois in the first game, winning 80-64. Zeller led five players in double figures with 24 points, and Oladipo posted another double-double with 12 points and 11 rebounds. The double-doubles back-to-back against Michigan and Illinois were two of Oladipo's three double-doubles for the season. The other came against Iowa in the conference opener.

IU's Big Ten run came to an end against the one program the Hoosiers just had not been able to beat – Wisconsin. The Badgers posted a 68-56 win against Indiana in the United Center as IU shot 38 percent from the field.

There are few IU players from that time period that have good memories of facing the Badgers. Hulls, Watford and Elston were 0-8 in their careers against Wisconsin. Oladipo was 0-6 and Zeller was 0-4.

"Disappointing. That's the only way you can describe it," Watford said. "It was just one of those things where they always seemed to play their best against us and we didn't respond. It's one of those things that is hard to figure out."

That loss sent Indiana to Selection Sunday with a 27-6 record and the belief that it had done enough that season to earn a No. 1 seed in the NCAA field. In just over 24 hours the Hoosiers would find out where they were seeded and where they were headed for the first round of the NCAA Tournament.

They hadn't been perfect throughout the regular season, but they had been pretty good.

Now, it was tournament time.

# Chapter 7

**O**n Selection Sunday, Indiana and head coach Tom Crean were rewarded for all of the hard work the program had endured since the dark days at the end of the Kelvin Sampson era.

The Hoosiers were given one of the four No. 1 seeds for just the third time in program history and sent to Dayton, Ohio and a game with No. 16-seed James Madison. IU's other No. 1 seeds in history had come in 1987 and 1993. (The NCAA stared seeded the full field of 64 in 1985.)

While IU did earn a No. 1 seed, it didn't earn the No. 1 overall tournament seed, and that was a huge distinction. Being first overall would have meant being placed in the Midwest regional staying home for the regional semifinals and finals games at Lucas Oil Stadium in Indianapolis. Instead, that honor went to Louisville and Indiana was placed in the East regional instead. The Hoosiers' route to the Final Four would take them through Dayton and Washington D.C., and not getting a chance to play in Indy was a disappointment to the Hoosiers.

"I felt like we had done enough to get the No. 1 seed overall and that's what we all really wanted because we wanted to stay close to home and ultimately be able to play in Indianapolis," IU senior forward Christian Watford said. "So we were happy to be a No. 1 seed, but disappointed that we didn't get the top spot overall.

"We just all felt that the top spot overall would have given us the best chance to win it all."

Yogi Ferrell said Selection Sunday was a great atmosphere with family and friends in attendance and the euphoria that was felt when IU saw that it had earned a No. 1 seed.

"It just felt right," Ferrell said. "It wasn't the No. 1 overall seed but we felt like we had left that in someone else's hands when we lost to Wisconsin in the Big Ten semifinals. But we also felt like a No. 1 seed was still going to give us a great chance to realize our dream, which was to hang another banner in Assembly Hall."

The stage was set. The location might not have been preferred, but the Hoosiers were ready to go.

A banner awaited. It would take six good nights.

***   ***   ***

**W**hen **Indiana faced** James Madison in the first game of the NCAA Tournament, one would have expected the Dukes had game-planned to stop Cody Zeller or Victor Oladipo. After all, those two players were just a few months removed from being NBA lottery picks. You might have even believed that James Madison had circled Christian Watford or Jordan Hulls as players that could take over the game if not given the proper attention.

Chances are, however, that Yogi Ferrell didn't garner the same level of respect. The freshman point guard was only shooting 30 percent from the field and averaging less than eight points per game. He was known as a pass-first, shoot-second type of player.

But as Hulls had said earlier in the year, one of the great things about this Indiana team was that someone was always there to step up when Indiana needed them the most.

Against No.16-seed James Madison, Ferrell saw an opening and it was as if a light went on in his head. The freshman point guard from Indianapolis scored IU's first nine points and 14 in the first six minutes. He finished with 16 points, eight rebounds and six assists to help lead the Hoosiers to a 83-62 victory. IU had five players in double figures and Watford was close with nine points.

When we say Ferrell saw an opening that's not an exaggeration. The first three times down the court, he simply drove straight to the basket scored.

"I was just trying to push the ball in transition really and find openings," Ferrell said. "The lane kind of just opened up for me, and I just kept attacking at the beginning. When they closed it up, I'd just kick out. So those first early drives really helped us."

In the postgame press conference, Crean talked about how much Ferrell had matured to that point in the season.

"He's just a very mature young man that's got an extremely short memory," Crean said. "He just plays, and he moves on, and he moves right on from it."

It was one down and five to go for the Hoosiers following the easy win over James Madison.

But that's when things stopped being easy.

***     ***     ***

**N**ext up was scrappy Temple and it looked like the top-seeded Hoosiers might not even make it to the Sweet Sixteen. IU had no answer for Temple guard Khalif Wyatt, who made shot after shot and consistently kept the Hoosiers in a hole.

Wyatt scored a game-high 31 points. In a low-scoring game, Temple held a 52-48 advantage with 2:56 to play and Hoosier fans were on the edge of their seats.

But in the game's final three minutes, Indiana's defense stiffened and Wyatt and his teammates were held scoreless down the stretch. Indiana closed the game on a 10-0 run and posted a 58-52 win that advanced it to Washington D.C. and a Sweet Sixteen game with Syracuse. IU led by one with 48 seconds to play and worked the ball down to two seconds on the shot clock before Oladipo sealed the deal with a three-pointer from the top of the arc with 14 seconds to play.

In the postgame press conference, Oladipo said the key for him was that he didn't really think about that shot. He just shot it. It was like muscle memory for him. It was the perfect illustration of how far he had come shooting the ball. The year before he was a 20 percent three-point shooter. In 2012-13, he shot 44.3 percent from beyond the arc.

"When the game is in movement and we hit Cody (Zeller) in the post, people get open shots," Oladipo said. "I was just moving without the ball. Cody found me, and I was open, and I just pretty much shot the ball. I was just open, and I shot it. It really didn't have anything to do with the moment or the confidence to shoot it. I just caught it and shot it. I didn't think about it."

Zeller said he believed IU's ability to keep its composure and score the final 10 points of the game was a product of how many close games the Hoosiers had played in during the regular season.

"That's what we've been doing all year," Zeller said at the time. "We've been in a lot of close games throughout the Big Ten especially. We've got a mature group that, even though it wasn't going as well, we wouldn't get things going for a while, but that's what winners do. You've got to survive and advance this time of year. We got some big plays down the stretch and we're lucky to be moving on."

Hulls said in the spring of 2015 that IU certainly wasn't looking past Temple in any way. He said they went into that game thinking the Owls were a solid team.

"The Temple game was definitely a challenge for us," Hulls said. "We knew going into the game they were a great team

**Mike Dickbernd/IU Athletics**

Cody Zeller was a key recruit for Tom Crean because he had been an Indiana prep legend and both older brothers had spurned IU for other schools. Zeller was exceptional in his two years in Bloomington.

110

who played well together and also had a great player in Wyatt. The NCAA Tournament is full of only good teams, so we didn't over look them at all."

Hulls believed it was a game where IU showed its true colors. Even in a scenario where the Hoosiers didn't shoot the ball particularly well (only 42 percent from the field), they still found a way to make the necessary plays in crunch time, a trait that Hulls believed was the mark of a championship quality team.

"When we needed a stop, we got one. When we needed a bucket we got one," Hulls said. "I'll never forget the shot Victor hit that sealed the game for us. We just overflowed with excitement, because with all the hard work we had put in we understood that anything could happen and that games can come down to one shot, one block, one rebound ... anything."

But Hulls' best memory from that game wasn't a good one, because he suffered a shoulder injury that limited his play.

"I was going for the ball when I suddenly got blindsided and collided with a Temple player," Hulls said. "I thought I had just got a stinger and it would feel fine in a little bit. As some possessions went by, that's when I knew something was wrong. It was hurting to dribble, pass, defend and I wasn't happy. I went back to the locker room with our medical staff and they tested my shoulder out. It was sore but no diagnosis could be made at the time, so I got a shot to get me through the pain just for the rest of the game because there was no way I was sitting out.

"It was a special game for me as I look back, because it was a testament to my heart. Nothing was going to keep me from helping my team win."

Nothing turned out to be something. Hulls had a partially torn pectoral muscle and a separated AC joint at the top of his shoulder.

Hulls' sore shoulder wasn't the only concern coming out of the Temple game. Watford said the narrow victory that required a huge comeback in the final minutes simply reinforced in his mind that all was not right with this Indiana basketball team. He couldn't put his finger on it, but something was different. Watford thought his team had lost its edge.

"We didn't really get burnt out, but we were going through a tough stretch," Watford said. "I could feel it as a senior. I shared those thoughts with our team at the end but we just never really got back on track. Jordy hurting his shoulder didn't help, but there were just issues within our team that are hard to explain. I don't know if it was a mental thing or what, but something was definitely different."

Others saw it as well.

"Personally, that week I wasn't able to practice at all," Derek Elston said. "The pain I was having in my knee was indescribable. It literally left me incapable of walking some days. From a team perspective, we were all just shocked Temple could do that to us.

"Without Vic's three-pointer and Christian's block at the end, we would have gone home feeling like we disappointed the world. Even after the win, we kind of had that same feeling. You have to be very lucky to win the national championship, but we weren't happy with the way we played."

Elston said that Oladipo, despite hitting the big three-pointer late, was visibly upset after the game, even after winning and leading the team in scoring with 16.

"Vic took most of the burden and you could just tell after the game something was wrong with him," Elston said. "The energy was as if we had just lost, when in the back of my mind I was thinking, 'OK, that didn't go the way we wanted it to, but who cares we won we are moving on.' I was thinking, 'Let's go home, let's get in the gym, let's work the kinks out and we will be good to go.' I didn't think it was a big deal.

"But that wasn't the case at all."

***  ***  ***

**M**att Roth didn't play at Indiana in the 2012-13 season. His last season had been the year before. But he remembered watching Selection Sunday and thinking that Indiana had gotten a real tough draw with the No. 4 seed in its region.

"You look at Selection Sunday and it comes down to all of your matchups," Roth said. "And they were the one seed that year and obviously anything short of a championship is going to be a disappointment, but you look at matchups and for being a No. 1, they probably got the toughest four-seed they possibly could. The way the NCAA Tournament works out with the top five seeds, is it really comes down to how their draw is."

Standing in IU's way in the first game of the Sweet Sixteen in Washington was a big, talented, athletic Syracuse team. Think of Syracuse and you think of a very difficult 2-3 zone defense. Former Georgetown coach John Thompson Jr. once referred to the defense as a "damn amoeba."

It's constantly changing and evolving and adapting to taking away the strength of each opponent. Jim Boeheim has utilized the defense for more than 30 years but it's filled with tweaks and little nuances that make it very difficult to prepare for.

For the Hoosiers, it was a struggle from the start.

Against Indiana, Syracuse did its best to front and take away Cody Zeller in the middle while the guards were trapping the ball each time it went to the wing. It made for difficult entry passes

113

as well as vulnerability in the perimeter passing lanes.

"They were just long and active," Oladipo said in the postgame press conference. "We just didn't take care of the ball like we should have. In the first half we got a little too anxious, catching the ball, moving out the ball, not having the ball secure in our hands, and our shots weren't falling at the same time. So that's pretty much it."

The beef from Hoosier Nation in the days, weeks, months and even years after that game was that IU coach Tom Crean had a week to prepare for Syracuse and yet the Hoosiers looked completely befuddled and unprepared.

Watford said it had nothing to do with being unprepared. If anything, he said looking back, it was that IU spent too much time in preparation worrying about the zone.

"Now that I look back on it, I think we were so worried about their zone and what they were going to do, that we weren't that much about our ourselves and the things that we needed to do," Watford said in a 2015 interview. "I think we put too much of an emphasis on it. We made it too much of a big deal, instead of just going out and doing what we do. We had a group of guys with great basketball IQ and I just wonder if maybe we were just a little too robotic when it came to attacking that zone.

"We were all caught up in the fact that the ball had to go here, here and here instead of trusting our instincts and just doing what had got us to that point that season."

Jordan Hulls said anyone that says that IU wasn't prepared for the Syracuse zone simply wasn't paying attention. He said that wasn't the case at all. Looking back in the spring of 2015, Hulls said Indiana had a good game plan, it simply didn't execute that night against Syracuse.

And it was 40 minutes of struggling to execute. Syracuse

won 61-50 but it wasn't even that close. The Orange led by nearly 20 in the first half and Indiana never did come up with an answer to contend.

"We just didn't play how we needed to in order to win," Hulls said. "We didn't make shots, didn't attack the zone as well as we needed to, never got in a rhythm and didn't defend them like we had to. It's so easy for us to look back now and analyze the film to see other ways to attack it, but it's what we thought was the best at the time and that's all that matters. Our coaches prepared us with a game plan they thought was best for us to win the game and we believed in them, just as we had all year long.

"You need a little break every now and then to win it all and we just didn't have it that game. We could've hit more shots, got more stops, got to the free throw line more. There are so many things that go through my mind, but what's done is done and we have to live with it."

Elston agreed wholeheartedly with Hulls that Indiana had a perfect game plan for Syracuse. It just didn't make shots. And when you don't make shots, on the biggest stage under the brightest lights, it's going to be very difficult to win deep in the NCAA Tournament.

"We watched that Louisville-Syracuse Big East championship game so many times we could have literally told you what play was next after every situation," Elston said. "It was the perfect example of how to defeat the zone and we ran it to perfection all week in practice. It's just very hard to emulate the length they have. Honestly, we were running our zone plays perfectly. But you still have to make shots."

When Elston thinks about that game, that's what comes to mind. IU's shooting was abysmal. The Hoosiers were 16-of-48 from the field, 33 percent. It was IU's lowest shooting percentage of the season. In 36 games, IU only had five games where it didn't shoot better than 40 percent. For the season, the Hoosiers hit 48.2 percent from the field.

IU also struggled from beyond the arc, hitting just three of 15 shots. That percentage was less than half of its season three-point percentage of 40.3 percent.

Everyone struggled. Zeller scored 10 points but did so on 3-of-11 shooting. Watford had 13 points but was 4-of-11 from the field.

IU turned it over 19 times, including 15 by the starters.

"Not hitting shots and finishing at the rim was a huge reason why they got the upper hand on us," Elston said. "If you watch the Syracuse-Michigan game you'll see our exact game plan. They just hit the shots that we didn't."

Syracuse coach Jim Boeheim said the plan was to attack Indiana's three-point shooters.

"Our defense has been good all year and I thought it was really good," Boeheim said in his postgame remarks. "Indiana presents a lot of problems offensively and we wanted to get on their three-point shooters. We did not want to let them get good looks and we did that."

\*\*\*     \*\*\*     \*\*\*

**B**oeheim, who lost the 1987 national championship game to Indiana, also knew he had a huge advantage at the guard spot. It would make a big difference on both ends of the floor.

"We made some really good defensive plays against them and offensively we wanted our guards to go on their little guards," he said. "That was the best way to play offensively in this game."

Piggybacking on Boeheim's comment about IU's "little

guards," Watford said in the spring of 2015, as he looked back at that game, that Syracuse posed a bad matchup not just in terms of the zone but in overall team make-up.

IU's guards, Hulls and Ferrell, were both just 6-foot and less than 180 pounds. Syracuse starters Michael Carter-Williams and Brandon Triche were 6-foot-6 and 6-foot-4, respectively, and both were quick with long arms.

That's a lot of size to be giving up and both too advantage of those matchups. Carter-Williams had 24 points and Triche had 14.

"They had big guards who were posting up Yogi and posting up Jordan," Watford said. "It makes a big difference in terms of the easy buckets they were getting. And then as far as the zone, they just neutralized us on the offensive end. We couldn't score the way we were used to scoring. The referees let them play a little more physical than we had seen anyone play against us all year. It was just a combination of things that added up to a real bad matchup for us."

Ferrell said Syracuse's combination of size and length in the zone were just too much for IU.

"They were long and not just with their bigs but with their wings, too," Ferrell said. "They just had long guys. If you penetrated they were coming to block it. It's just hard to be successful against that zone because they were so long."

Ken Bikoff, the longtime IU beat writer for both Inside Indiana and Peegs.com, believed that Syracuse's length was the biggest issue.

"It was a bad matchup from the time it was announced on Selection Sunday," Bikoff said. "That was the game you could easily point to and see IU was going to have trouble. Syracuse's zone is always a headache, but throw in the lack of size in the backcourt with Jordan and Yogi, and that put IU at a real disadvantage. Indiana struggled to get the ball inside, the length and athleticism were tough to handle for a team that was already tired, and IU didn't shoot the ball particularly well, either. It was a bad matchup from a physical standpoint, and the fact the bad physical matchup also played zone was an issue IU couldn't overcome."

Jake Query, the Indianapolis radio talk show host on WNDE 1260-AM, said he thought Indiana's problems against Syracuse were as much rooted in fatigue as anything Syracuse was able to do in the Sweet Sixteen.

"To me the issue was simple: Crean practiced them as hard, if not harder, in March than in January," Query said. "That team was spent. They were gassed. Victor Oladipo, he of extreme work ethic and athleticism, was walking up the floor in the last minutes of that game (against Syracuse). He was walking. A matchup zone requires attention to detail, mental sharpness, focus and energy to defeat. Indiana had none of it."

Query said there's great irony in those who want to point to Crean and say he didn't have IU prepared to play Syracuse. Query believes fatigue was the bigger factor.

"The irony of the critique of the 2013 team is this," Query said. "They weren't UNDER-coached. They were OVER-coached."

*** *** ***

**T**he mismatch at the guard spot couldn't have been more pronounced. Carter-Williams and Triche combined for 38 points.

Hulls and Ferrell combined for ... ZERO.

The same Jordan Hulls that scored 1,318 points in an Indiana uniform and 348 in his senior year, came up empty in the final

118

game of his college career. He missed all six of his shots, and all were from beyond the arc. He finished with zero points.

And for the second game in a row, Ferrell was missing in action. Ferrell didn't score in the narrow Temple win and he was shut out again against Syracuse. He missed all four of his shot attempts against, and had seven turnovers. Against Syracuse he had one assist and four turnovers – and no points. And that was in a combined 55 minutes of action.

Looking back on it three years later, Ferrell admitted that he wasn't himself.

"I was nervous," Ferrell said in the summer of 2015. "I was a nervous freshman. I was. And looking back – and especially the way I play now – I get so mad at myself because I played scared. And I should never play scared. Ever. But I was a freshman on a big stage, with big lights and a big environment. I felt like that whole game was much my fault as anyone else's."

Hulls said it wasn't a lack of confidence as much as a lack of execution.

"Syracuse was a team that was unlike any other team we had faced all year," Hulls said. "They were long, athletic, and very talented guys who played their system very well. There was never a doubt in our minds that we could beat Syracuse. We believed we could and that we would. Obviously it wasn't going to be easy, games at that level never are.

"We just didn't do enough things to give ourselves a chance."

\*\*\*     \*\*\*     \*\*\*

Roth said that while some fans may think the year was a disappointment, he doesn't look at it that way. And in essence, since he wasn't on that team, he was a fan. A very educated fan but still a fan.

"Syracuse has been good for a really long time playing that zone," Roth said. "Long before I was born, they were playing it. It has obviously worked for a great deal of time for Syracuse and it has happened to a lot of teams that have run into that zone and it's frustrating because you think a zone defense should be easy to break but when you put the size, athleticism and talent that Syracuse had, it was a really difficult matchup.

In his postgame remarks following the loss to Syracuse, Crean talked about how proud he was of the young men in his program, and all they had endured to bring IU back to national prominence.

"Well, we have had a heck of a ride with this group, and it doesn't feel like that tonight, won't feel like that for a couple of days, maybe longer," Crean said.

"But the bottom line is that this program has come from so far and I hope at some point in time, the seniors, the guys on this team, will remember that they did things that hadn't been done, first off in 20 years at Indiana, but more importantly there are not any programs – whether this be Syracuse, Kentucky, Carolina, Duke, you name it – that are the blue-blood programs in the country that have had to endure what these guys have had to endure. They have done it with perseverance, toughness, and improvement and they have done it with great class and they will all be better for it."

Dave Furst, the sports anchor for WRTV-Channel 6 in Indianapolis, remembers the shocked faces he encountered in the IU locker room that night in Washington D.C.

"I don't ever remember a game where one team's scheme so dominated a night," Furst said. "Syracuse's zone is good. But

that night, it was an instructional video. I also don't remember
a locker room as stunned as that one was after the game. It was
already a late night after a late tip in DC and I couldn't imagine
anyone on that team sleeping well after that performance."

*** *** ***

**T**wo years later, in the spring of 2015, a few players on
that team were asked to reflect on the way it had ended. Specifically, how long had it taken to get past the feeling that in losing to
Syracuse and not advancing further in the NCAA Tournament the
Hoosiers had potentially let a great opportunity get away.

All of the answers were extremely insightful. Of course,
the seniors ached the most.

"For as long as I live, I will never get over that game,"
Hulls said. "I hate losing more than anything, even more than winning. All I remember from after the game is frustration and sad-
ness, saying to myself, 'It's really over. I'll never play for Indiana
University again. I'll never wear the candy stripes and run out of
the tunnel in Assembly Hall in front of a sold out crowd. I missed
every shot in the final game of my career. Why did I have to hurt
my shooting shoulder against Temple? What could I have done
better? I let my team down.'

Hulls said his mind was filled with those kinds of thoughts
and emotions. He said he then had to speak to the media in the
locker room at the Verizon Center for one last time and that didn't
help at all.

From there, the team headed back to the hotel.

"Going back to the hotel, I was in shock still," Hulls said.
"I roomed with Cody Zeller on the road and we had become real
close. We just kept talking about the 'coulda, shoulda, woulda's'

and how we couldn't believe it was all over. We all truly believed this was our year to win it all, we had all the pieces, but it just wasn't meant to be. It was one of the longest nights of my life."

Hulls was asked if he has ever gone back and watched the Syracuse game. He answer was quick and to the point.

"I have not gone back to watch the game," Hulls said, "and I never will."

Elston said he remembers the next morning at the hotel when the team ate together before they boarded the bus to head for the airport. He said it was interesting scene.

"For some, NBA workouts were in the near future and for others I think they were happy that it was over because the pressure was starting to get to a few of the players and it wasn't the same group of guys like we all knew," Elston said.

Ferrell was in a little bit of a different situation because he still had three years of eligibility remaining. But even he said it was really difficult to get past that loss to the Orange.

"It took a while. It definitely took all summer," Ferrell said. "That offseason, I worked hard, and I wanted to come back with a chip on my shoulder. I think what hurt the most was knowing I would never play with those particular guys again and we just missed out on something that could have been really special."

Watford said he still isn't over the Syracuse loss, more than two years later. He then said he was kidding, but it didn't sound like he was.

"We still talk about it," Watford said. "Every time we're together, we all know that we should have hung a national championship banner in Assembly Hall and we talk about it. I don't feel like our season was a failure because we did do some great things and had a lot of high moments.

"But at the same time, we do feel like we let one slip

away."

***   ***   ***

**The naysayers in Indiana** – and there are a lot of them in the Tom Crean era – would say this 2013 team has no business being included on this list of great IU teams that didn't win a title.

Their argument would be that IU barely beat Temple in the second round and got slaughtered by Syracuse. Even if they had won, they still would have needed to win three more games against very good teams to win a championship.

But let's connect the dots. Louisville won the title that year, beating Michigan in the finals 82-76. Michigan came very close to winning a title themselves, and felt like they could have won, according to Glenn Robinson III, an Indiana kid from St. John who started on that team as a freshman and now plays with the Indiana Pacers in the NBA.

That Michigan team lost twice to Indiana during the regular season.

Dots connected?

"Well, I can't say anything bad about Indiana, because they did beat us twice," Robinson said in a lengthy 2015 interview. "We felt like we should have won that title, and if they beat us twice, I'm sure they think they could have won one, too.

"But if I had to choose, I'll take our tournament run over losing those two regular season games to Indiana every day. Every single day."

Robinson also has good perspective on dealing with Syracuse during that tournament. Michigan crushed them early in the national semifinal and then hung on for a 61-56 win.

"We obviously watched a lot of Indiana-Syracuse tape in

123

getting ready for that game and it was like night and day," Robin-son said. "I really felt like Indiana let Syracuse push them around. They didn't get good shots, and they didn't make much. We did, and we made them. We were much better prepared, I thought. Hav-ing seen so much of Indiana all year, they sure didn't look like the same team against Syracuse. They weren't very good that day.

"I'm sure they hated ending their season that way. We're rivals and they did some things we didn't like that year – like that Oladipo dunk at the end of the game in Bloomington and beating us the last day of the season for the Big Ten title – so we didn't mind seeing them lose in the NCAAs. But it also helped us pre-pare. We knew how to beat Syracuse and we learned that by watch-ing what Indiana didn't do. Plus we had seniors on our bench,

**Courtesy Hudson's Photo/Jordan & Aubrey Hulls**
Indiana traditions like banners and candy stripes do live on forever, as evidenced at Jordan Hulls' wedding in the summer of 2015. Hulls and his friends and teammates had to dress up one more time.

guys who had lost starting jobs to all us young guys, and they were a great scout team. They prepared us well for Syracuse. Indiana didn't look as prepared to me."

What Indiana *didn't* do. Sadly, that's so true. And that's something that has to be lived with forever.

**PhotoShop Created Image**
Most of the players on Indiana's 1993 team had played in the Final Four in 1992. They spent much of the '93 season ranked No. 1 in the country.

Chapter **8**

**M**any of the biggest disappointments in Indiana basketball history have been tempered by immediate elixirs. For instance,
the devastation of 1975 was followed by a national championship
in 1976. Same with 1980. That tough finish was followed by the
joyous title in 1981. For every title that got away, that massive pain
was replaced by the over-the-top joy that comes from winning a
national championship.

But the 1992 and 1993 seasons were different. Dramatical-
ly different, and for one very painful reason. IU's 1992 team came
so close to winning a national title – getting jobbed by referee Ted
Valentine and his colleagues against a very good Duke team at
the Final Four – and had an even better chance to win the following year in 1993, only to come up short after losing one of its best
players to a knee injury on the eve of the NCAA tournament.

There was no potion to take away the pain of '92, only
more pain in '93, literally and figuratively.

Those two title runs were made, for the most part, by the
same group of people. The coaching staff was the same and the
huge majority of points and rebounds were accounted for by mostly the same group of legendary IU players. Both years are easily
intertwined. It made for lengthy discussions and debate when we
discussed the parameters of this project as to which team to include
in our five. The discussion, and rightly so, centered for the longest
time on including them *both*.

They were each that awesome.

Although both teams certainly were capable of winning

127

titles, it seemed repetitive to discuss both years at great length because the actors were all the same. So we tried to come up with the team that was the most talented and most likely *should have* won a title.

It wasn't easy.

"That isn't an easy call, that's for sure," said Dan Dakich, the former IU player who was an assistant coach to Bob Knight during those two seasons and is now a popular radio host in Indianapolis and color commentator on college basketball broadcasts for ESPN. "The '92 team, by the end of the season they were really, really good but they weren't good all year. The '93 team was great all season and what they did in the Big Ten that year was impressive as hell. To go 17-1 is something, especially in such a loaded league that was filled with great players at that time. The Big Ten was awesome that season, maybe one of the best Big Ten years ever. And we totally dominated.

"That extra year of maturity was big with the '93 team. They were above all the nonsense, or stuff with Coach Knight or other teams. They were smart guys, seasoned, and they all liked each other so well."

The decision came down to this: Even though the '92 team advanced one game further in the tournament, what the '93 team did all year bordered on historic. They blew through the Big Ten like the legendary 1975 and 1976 teams did 17 years earlier and there was no doubt among the players that they were the best team in the country. Then star big man Alan Henderson blew out his knee in practice in late February and that was that.

"We were the best team in the country before Alan got hurt, and I say that with no doubt in my mind. The numbers proved it that year," IU legend Damon Bailey said in a 2015 interview. "I had no doubt then and I have no doubt now. We were that good."

So, for our purposes, 1993 it is.

"That's not wrong," Dakich said. "Forced to choose, I'd probably do the same. That's a tough one to split though, because both of those teams were really special. That was probably the best group I was ever around in all my years at Indiana. They would go to work and listen to Coach Knight."

Much like some of their predecessors, the heartbreak of 1992 fueled everything that went into that '93 season. They worked extremely hard and made great individual sacrifices for the greater good, hoping for a better final result. The '93 team was so good – and so incredibly focused – because of all they went through in 1992.

So, of course, we can't tell the story of the 1993 Indiana Hoosiers without telling a little bit about that wild 1992 season that was filled with some of the greatest highs in IU basketball history.

And some of the lowest lows.

*** *** ***

There was plenty of excitement surrounding the 1992 Hoosiers when the season rolled around. The previous year had been entertaining, with IU posting a 29-5 record and tying for the Big Ten title thanks to five straight wins down the stretch. An 83-65 shellacking at the hands of Kansas in the regional semifinals was a difficult and emphatic end to the season, but hopes were high in '92.

Calbert Cheaney was a junior then, and the clear superstar on the team. Eric Anderson was a senior, and youngsters Damon Bailey and the two Grahams, Greg and Pat, were all stars in their own right. IU won a huge recruiting war for 6-foot-9 Alan Hender-

129

**IU Archives P0056045**

The best rivalry in college basketball in 1992 and 1993 was between Indiana and Michigan's "Fab Five." IU's Alan Henderson (right) and Michigan's Chris Webber had some epic battles. IU won three of four games.

son, and they were loaded.

They also were all great friends, which wasn't a surprise at all. They had been playing together for years as kids, and through all those years a special bond was formed.

"We were really that first group that emerged from playing AAU ball together all the time," said Bailey, who was a sophomore then. "It's much more common now, but it was pretty rare back then. Calbert and I, Pat Graham and Greg Graham and even Alan later, we all played a lot of games together before we ever even got to IU. Chris Lawson, who started with us at Indiana but transferred later, he played AAU with us too. We all basically grew up together."

"When we got to IU, our roles were sort of already established, and that's really rare for college kids. I mean, we knew Calbert was the best player because we had played with him so much. We all understood what we could contribute when we got there because we knew each other so well. Other than Matt Nover and Chris Reynolds, the entire core of those teams played together for years. And we knew we were going to be capable of doing some good things while we were there."

Everyone was expecting good things. The Hoosiers were ranked No. 2 in the Associated Press preseason poll, the highest in school history at the time other than the two No. 1's by the 1976 and 1980 teams. (IU would be preseason No. 1 again in 2013.)

But the season started with a thud, an 87-72 pounding by No. 11-ranked UCLA in the Tipoff Classic in Springfield, Mass. It was a thrashing, and a real eye-opener for the players. They weren't a cocky bunch by nature anyway, but still it was a humbling experience. They knew they had plenty of work to do.

"Yep, we got our ass kicked by UCLA," Dakich said. "Lost by 15 and it wasn't even close. I think that was a good wake-up call for every one of them."

Nice in-state wins over Butler and Notre Dame followed, but then the Hoosiers fell to 2-2 after a heartbreaking 76-74 loss to No. 14-ranked Kentucky in a sold-out RCA Dome in Indianapolis.

But then they got hot. They won the seven remaining non-conference games in style, winning all but one by at least 17 points. A five-point win over No. 10-ranked St. John's at Madison Square Garden was the only close game. Most were routs.

When the Big Ten season started, IU was back in the top five in the national rankings. Cheaney had been spectacular and that continued in conference play. They opened with wins over Minnesota and Wisconsin and then beat No. 4-ranked Ohio State 91-83 in an epic battle in Assembly Hall. They won easily at Northwestern, came home and beat Michigan's Fab Five freshmen (Chris Webber, Jalen Rose, Juwan Howard, Ray Jackson and Jimmy King). The Hoosiers won 89-74 over the 16th-ranked Wolverines.

IU then went to 6-0 in the Big Ten with a 106-65 drubbing of Purdue, which was very sweet. (Isn't it always?). It was very clear the Hoosiers were getting better every day. The Boilermakers had no answers for them.

"I think our progress in '92 was more from a maturation for us as college players. We just kept getting better and better as that year rolled along," Bailey said. "It's a big jump going from high school to college, especially when you're playing at the level we're playing at and competing with the best in the country for a national championship. Calbert and them were juniors, but I was a sophomore and Alan was just a freshman. Every game we played, it just seemed like that experience just helped us keep getting better. We had so many weapons."

They took their first loss at Michigan State (76-60) and

then lost again at Minnesota three games later to fall to 8-2 in the league. They won five in a row then – including wins over ranked teams Michigan State and Ohio State – before losing at Michigan 68-60. IU beat Wisconsin, which set up a season-ending showdown with Purdue.

There was a lot on the line. Ohio State would finish 15-3 in the Big Ten and all Indiana needed was a win at Purdue to finish with the same record and grab its share of the conference title. Playing on the road in the Big Ten is tough, but IU showed up confident, firmly remembering its thorough 106-65 whipping of Purdue in Bloomington a month earlier.

And then they laid a massive egg.

Purdue won 61-59, and what an expensive loss it was for the Hoosiers. First off, losing to Purdue is never fun … and never acceptable. Losing out on a Big Ten title was bothersome, too. But what riled coach Bob Knight most was the way IU had played. It was, at least since the season opener, their worst effort of the year. And they got ripped for it. Some who have been around Indiana basketball a long time say it was one of the all-time Knight meltdowns in the locker room.

He was that angry.

"Yeah, the loss at Purdue was an all-time rip job," said Dakich, who witnessed every high-decibel word. "After that, I tell you, they were mature enough to handle it but they were also scared enough. No one ever wanted to lose another game again.

"Coach was so pissed. I mean, it was Purdue and we showed up there with no effort. I didn't get pissed very often, but I was really pissed off that day, too. Everybody was. Whatever Coach was going to do to punish then, I was all for it. Hell, I was even ready to run. That loss should have never happened. There was nothing Coach Knight hated more than losing because the

133

IU Archives P-0056041

Indiana forward Calbert Cheaney became the Big Ten's all-time leading scorer for a good reason, because he was not only an excellent shooter, but he could get to the rim as well.

other team played harder than we did. He just absolutely hated that."

The players remember it the same way. "I'll tell you what. He really lit into us," Cheaney said a few years ago. "That was a tough loss, a tough loss. But it lit a fire under our butts."

"We were really down," Henderson said a few years ago. "We had a lot of meetings, just as a team, to get things straight as far as our leadership and what direction we wanted to go in the tournament."

Another massive expense of the Purdue loss was that it cost the Hoosiers a No. 1 seed in the NCAA tournament. Instead they got a No. 2 seed, and had to go out west. They played their first two games in desolate Boise, Idaho, beating Eastern Illinois in the first round and LSU, featuring freshman Shaquille O'Neal, in the second round. The Hoosiers won with 6-8 Matt Nover giving up about five inches and 100 pounds to O'Neal.

O'Neal scored 36 points and had 12 rebounds but Nover went down in IU lore for battling O'Neal every step of the way in the 89-79 victory.

"I'm kind of known for being like the Dan Dakich who shut down Michael Jordan (in 1984), although I think Dakich was a little more effective at actually shutting Jordan down," Nover said with a laugh in a 2011 interview. "Everybody says I 'held' Shaq down and I think what I 'held' him to was about (36 and 12). It was definitely his last college game."

They advanced to the West regional in Albuquerque, N.M., and beat Florida State 85-74 in the semifinals. It set up a regional final with No. 1-seed UCLA, the same team that started IU's season with a 15-point beatdown.

This time, it also wasn't close. But this time, it was all Indiana. The Hoosiers won 106-79 to earn a trip to the Final Four in

135

Minneapolis. Payback was sweet. It was also a great sign as to far these team had progressed through the course of the season. They were playing at a very high level, and at the right time.

The win earned them a date with the defending champion and No. 1-ranked Duke Blue Devils, a team that was loaded with stars at every position, including Christian Laettner, Grant Hill, Bobby Hurley, Brian Davis and Thomas Hill.

But it would be Ted Valentine who would be remembered forever.

Referee Ted Valentine.

*** *** ***

**IU Archives P-0056033**
IU basketball coach Bob Knight was into the sweater look by 1993 but one thing hadn't changed at all. He still disagreed often with officials.

**All eyes were on** Indiana and Duke in the national semi-final. There were storylines galore, the biggest being the coaching battle between Bob Knight and Duke's Mike Krzyzewski. Coach K had played for Knight at Army, then coached there after Knight had left for Indiana. Knight was also instrumental in Krzyzewski getting hired at Duke in 1980

Everyone also was pretty convinced that these were the two best teams in the country at the moment, with no disrespect intended for the other semifinalists, Michigan and Cincinnati. There were stars all over the floor in the IU-Duke showdown.

And Indiana dominated early. The Hoosiers got up by double digits and led 39-27 at one point. Their defense had been stifling. Twelve minutes in, Indiana had been called for only four fouls and it looked like an upset in the making. Everything was falling into place nicely for Indiana. Duke's star, college basketball legend and bad boy Christian Laettner, would score only eight points the entire game.

But within the next 12 minutes, Calbert Cheaney, Alan Henderson and Damon Bailey all had four fouls called against them. The game basically ground to a halt, with fouls seemingly being called on every Duke possession. During the final 28 minutes of the game, Indiana was called for 29 fouls. During that same time, Duke was called for only 11. Cheaney, Henderson, Bailey and Greg Graham would all foul out. Bailey got called for his third and fourth fouls in a span *of four seconds*. Duke shot 42 free throws to Indiana's 16 and went on a crazy 26-2 run in the second half, finally winning 81-78.

It wasn't that close until the very end. Todd Leary hit three late three-pointers in about 30 seconds for Indiana to narrow the gap but Jamal Meeks missed the last shot that could have tied it.

Leary went nuts and almost created a miracle.

His three three-pointers came in a 24-second period, turning a double-digit deficit into a one-possession game. Indiana trailed by three and had a chance to tie in the closing seconds, but IU couldn't get the ball to Leary and Jamal Meeks attempted a long three-pointer but it was off and Duke won, 81-78.

Cheaney smiled a few years back when reminiscing about Leary's flurry of three-pointers. Does he wish that Leary had gotten the ball at the end to have one more shot at a fourth three-pointer to send the game into overtime?

"Without a doubt," Cheaney said. "We had all fouled out so we didn't have much of a say in it. But absolutely, we wish he had hit one more shot to force overtime. If you could get to overtime, you never know what might have happened. But that was unbelievable. It was an unbelievable individual display of shooting and something you don't see every day."

It was tough watching the final minutes of that game from the bench, with Cheaney and several other starters out of the game with fouls. How the game was officiated was very frustrating to everybody.

"In the second half, with the way they were making those calls, it was like you had to play with your hands in your pocket," Cheaney said a few years ago. "Because if you touched anybody, you were going to get called for a foul."

Cheaney said at one point he tried to get an explanation from Valentine, but he gave him nothing but a threat of a technical foul.

The technical foul, that would come later.

After IU's lead was lost and Duke was starting to pull away, Bailey broke free for a lay-up. He hesitated a bit, hoping to get contact from Grant Hill and a potential three-point play. Hill clobbered Bailey on his way up to the basket, but no foul was called and the Indiana bench jumped up in disbelief.

That's when Teddy V. stepped in.

Valentine called a technical on the bench. Knight went nuts. Duke made the free throws, scored again and the game was basically over.

Knight was incredulous over the technical after the game. When asked about it at the time, he said. "The official told Cheaney that the technical was called because the bench jumped up. Those were his exact words. All I'll say is that's the first and only time I've ever been assessed a technical – or seen any called on anyone – for the bench jumping up."

To this day, Bailey remains steadfast in giving Duke its props. The Blue Devils would crush Michigan two nights later for the title.

But still …

"Duke was very good and they were in the middle of a great run, so I'll never want to make it sound like I'm taking anything away from them," Bailey said in a 2015 interview. "They were a great team and we knew it would take a great effort to beat them, but we absolutely were convinced we could beat them if we played well. But we didn't, especially in the second half. I know a lot of people have complained about the officiating after that, but that's just part of the game. You have to try to overcome all of that, and we didn't do it. For as good as we were playing coming into that game, we didn't play up to that same standard in that game."

Dakich remembers his blood boiling not long after that game. The coaching staff, Knight included, felt like they were robbed. Sure, IU could have played better, but the officiating absolutely was a factor in how that game played out.

"Losing that game to Duke was tough. Sure, we thought the officiating was brutal," Dakich said. "I remember after the

IU Archives P-0056031

Guard Damon Bailey (22) came to Indiana as one of the most talked-about recruits in the history of the program. He didn't disappoint, leaving IU as one of its all-time favorite players as well.

game, (IU assistant coach) Ron Felling and I are sitting there bitching and moaning and (national TV announcer) Billy Packer comes up to us and says the officiating 'had no effect on the game.' I never wanted to beat the shit out of someone more than I wanted to beat the shit out of Billy Packer that night.

"But Duke deserved their props, too. Bobby Hurley simply refused to lose that game. He made one big shot after another and that Duke defense had become impenetrable. They really guarded, and we had great scorers all over the floor. You had to tip your hat to Duke. They won back-to-back titles and they were really, really good."

The anger level between Knight and Valentine was so bad that Big Ten management kept the two of them apart for six years after that Duke game. Valentine did Big Ten games most every week all those years, but never any of Indiana's games.

And when they were finally reunited for the first time, it was even worse. Knight got thrown out of the game, went berserk and was eventually fined $10,000 for being so out of control.

The loss to Duke was a tough one to swallow for the players. But they would come back the next year ready to contend again. That's what they do.

"That's why you come to Indiana, to go to Final Fours and compete for titles," Bailey said. "That next year, we had every intention of doing the same thing. With what we had coming back, we were sure we'd have another shot at getting it right the next time."

Getting another shot. That's what mattered. The shot in '92 got away from them. So close, but not quite close enough.

"The '92 team should have won it because of the way they played in the tournament," longtime Bloomington Herald-Times sports editor Bob Hammel said during a 2015 interview. "They had

141

a cold spot at the end of that tournament and they were basically awful (in Duke's wild 26-2 run). They just couldn't shoot and they all got in foul trouble.

"Calbert (Cheaney) and I talked about it years later and he always looked back at that game and just shook his head because it was the one performance that just didn't add up with the rest of that season."

He would get another chance, but this one still really hurt. That '92 team was special, and everyone knew it.

"That was probably the best team I was on for the entire four years I was there," Cheaney said. "We had a great year my senior year in 1993, but we were much deeper my junior year. We had so many guys who could come off the bench and do so many things for us.

"For us to go to the Final Four and then have a tough game against Duke, it was definitely disappointing. It's one of those things, where to win a national championship, the breaks have to go your way. And the breaks didn't go our way that particular night."

# Chapter 9

**Another year older**, another year wiser. And ten times as hungry.

That's how the Hoosiers approached the 1993 season. Coming close in 1992 was one thing, but what those Indiana players liked most about that team was how it continued to get better every day.

That was the same challenge in '93. The roster was loaded with experienced talent and everyone knew their roles. Lots of teams have a goal of winning a national title in November each year, but for this group of Hoosiers, those dreams seemed very real.

It could be a special season, with a special group of players.

"They had no egos, which is saying something considering how highly publicized they were before they got there," said former IU assistant coach Dan Dakich, who was on Bob Knight's staff at the time. "I mean, no one ever walked onto a college campus with more pub than Damon Bailey, and Alan Henderson was a huge recruit, too. Calbert Cheaney, too. But these were really good, really smart kids and they were great leaders. And they worked."

They also had plenty of weapons. For instance, during the 1992 and 1993 seasons, the Hoosiers were so balanced that they had five guys average in double figures in scoring. It's the only time in school history that's been done in consecutive years. It had never happened before and it has never happened since.

Winning it all was the only thought on their mind.

"Going to Indiana, you always feel you're going to have a

legitimate chance to go to the Final Four," said IU guard Damon Bailey, who was a junior that season. "Every player that goes to school wants to win a national championship, but when you go to Indiana or Kentucky or Duke or Kansas, you expect to go there and be one of the top teams in the country. I was the same way at Indiana. I expected to go to Final Fours, expected to have a chance to win a national championship."

The Hoosiers, who were ranked No. 4 in the Associated Press preseason poll, were pushed right from the start with a very difficult schedule. They were part of the 16-team preseason NIT tournament and started the season by winning the first two games on campus against Murray State and No. 17-ranked Tulane to advance to New York City, where two top 10 teams awaited them.

IU dispatched No. 7-ranked Florida State 81-78 in overtime in the semifinals, but not without a price. Pat Graham, who had dealt with several foot injuries throughout his IU career, injured the foot again and it would require surgery that would involve nearly three months of rehab. In the finals, the Hoosiers beat No. 6-ranked Seton Hall 78-74 to win the prestigious event, a first for a Big Ten team.

When the Associated Press poll came out the following week, IU stood at 4-0 was up to No. 2 in the country.

As if that wasn't battle enough early in the season, the Hoosiers then faced No. 3-ranked Kansas in a huge nationally-televised showdown at the RCA Dome in Indianapolis, which drew more than 31,000 fans and had many buzzing about it being a potential Final Four preview.

Both teams were that good. And even that early in the season, the game deserved all its hype.

The game lived up to its billing. Indiana played well early and jumped out to a 40-31 late in the first half. Cheaney had been sensational, scoring 12 early points, but he sat out the final minutes of the half with two fouls. So did sophomore Alan Henderson, who also had two. Kansas made IU pay with a flurry of points before halftime and when the Jayhawks scored on the first possession of the second half, they had the lead.

The game went back and forth throughout the second half, with IU never leading by more than five and Kansas never getting any further ahead than six.

IU pushed ahead 69-66 lead with 3:30 left, but they wouldn't score again. Kansas scored the final eight points of the game to win 74-69.

It was a tough shooting day for the Hoosiers. After making 5 of 6 three-pointers in the first half, they missed all nine attempts from beyond the arc in the second half.

They also were bad at the free throw line. IU made only 4 of 13 freebies and missed the front end of several one-and-one opportunities. Kansas was 15-for-20 from the line, a huge difference. Free throws were the difference.

Indiana got back to its winning ways three nights later with a 75-70 win at Notre Dame, but it wasn't pretty. IU blew a 17-point lead and once again missed a bunch of free throws. A Matt Nover jumper late sealed the deal.

IU won its next six nonconference games easily and was 11-1 when it faced No. 3-ranked Kentucky on Jan. 3 at Freedom Hall in Louisville. It was a strange game in the packed arena.

Kentucky attempted a whopping 41 three-pointers, making 16 in beating Indiana 81-78. It spoiled great nights by Hoosiers Calbert Cheaney and Matt Nover, who had 29 points each. IU shot 56 percent from the field compared to 39 percent for UK, but it was at the free throw line once again where IU struggled. They did a great job of getting to the line, but they made only 18 of 36 at-

IU Archives P-0056042

Calbert Cheaney (40) puts up a shot during a game at Assembly Hall in 1993. Cheaney was named the National Player of the Year in 1993. The Evansville native is still Indiana's all-time leading scorer.

tempts and missed the front end of four one-and-ones.

The Big Ten season awaited, but it seemed like the jury was still out on how good this IU team was going to be. They were 11-2 and had nice wins against ranked opponents Tulane, Florida State, Seton Hall and Cincinnati.

But the two heavyweights on their nonconference schedule, Kansas and Kentucky, both got the measure of the Hoosiers.

Just how good were they? We would soon find out.

*** *** ***

**What IU did during the** Big Ten season in 1993 hadn't been matched since the great Hoosiers teams of 1975 and 1976 that went undefeated in league play. They threatened running the table themselves, finishing 17-1 in a league loaded with great teams and great players.

They had massive battles along the way, but none bigger than with Michigan. The Wolverines might have been one of the most hyped teams in college basketball history. They were the "Fab Five," five freshmen who all came in together and practically singlehandedly changed the fabric of college basketball. They brought swagger to a new level. They unveiled the long, baggy shorts and black socks and they strutted their stuff whenever they could. They had great players like Chris Webber and Juwan Howard and Jalen Rose and as freshmen they had made it all the way to the NCAA title game, losing to the Duke team that had knocked out Indiana in the Final Four semifinals.

And as much as IU talked about national titles in 1993, it was Michigan that hogged most of the national spotlight. This was to be their year of coronation. They were the big kids on the block.

They also lost – twice – to Indiana during the regular sea-

147

son. And the Hoosiers loved every minute of that.

Their first meeting was on Jan. 12 in Ann Arbor. IU had opened the Big Ten season with two wins at home, beating No. 8 Iowa and Penn State to go to 13-2. The Wolverines were next, the start of a brutal three-games-in-eight-days road trip that also included games at Illinois and Purdue. Michigan was 12-1 and the entire country couldn't wait for the IU-Michigan showdown.

They didn't disappoint.

Indiana won 76-75 in a game where people were on the edge of their seats in Crisler Arena the entire night. It was that kind of battle. Indiana had jumped out to a 10-point lead early in the second half but Michigan roared right back to tie it at 45. From there, it was a 15-minute battle to the finish. Neither team could get ahead by more than four points.

And once it got to 64-63, neither team could get ahead by more than a basket. The lead kept changing with every basket as the clock wound down. Sophomore Alan Henderson, valiantly battling against Webber and Howard inside all night, was spectacular. He finished with a game-high 22 points and five blocked shots, the biggest one coming right before the buzzer with IU clinging to that 76-75 lead. Webber got a rebound and went up for the game-winner, but Henderson got a piece of the ball and slapped it away. IU hung on for a huge win.

All involved used every glowing adjective available to describe how great the game was. Even Michigan coach Steve Fisher said the game "was expertly played" by two great teams. No one would argue.

The Hoosiers would continue to roll through the Big Ten. They won at Illinois and then traveled to Purdue for a much-anticipated showdown with Glenn Robinson and the Boilermakers. Robinson was Mr. Basketball in Indiana in 1991 and had won a super-hyped battle with Alan Henderson in the state championship game. Robinson had to sit out his freshman year at Purdue for academic reasons, so this was his first college battle with Henderson at the rival schools.

The matchup drew plenty of pregame hype, which was understandable. But the battle of big men – won by Robinson – took a back seat to the Calbert Cheaney show. Cheaney scored 33 points and the Hoosiers won in Mackey Arena 74-65.

Knight had a great line at the time. He knew this game wasn't about Robinson vs. Henderson, even though that was the storyline that was used all week in the lead-up to the game.

``This will be Calbert's game," he said at the time. "They don't have anybody who can handle him. Nobody does.''

He was right about that.

Indiana then came home and destroyed No. 24 Ohio State by 27 points, 96-69. They beat Minnesota at home, then won road games at Northwestern and No. 9 Iowa before traveling to lowly Penn State.

They got a shocking scare that night, pulling out an 88-84 win in double overtime. Freshman Brian Evans was the hero that night for the first time, hitting a jumper near the end of the second OT to seal the deal.

A few years ago, Evans recalled that interesting night. He was a hero, but didn't really get to celebrate.

"Playing at Rec Hall (on the Penn State campus) was like no other venue. It looked like the court is half-size because the students are right on it," he said. "Coach put me in during the second half and I shot an air ball, so he took me out immediately. But as people kept fouling out, he was going through his bench. At the end of the first overtime, Greg Graham fouled out, so I went in. The play wasn't designed for me, but Coach always was in favor of us coming down and just running our offense. At the eight-second mark I took a couple of dribbles and shot a 12-footer from the baseline with a guy's hand in my face.

"I had just hit this big shot and thought I would go into the locker room and be mobbed by my teammates. But Coach was livid, thought we played like crap. He went to the press conference and said he was rooting for Penn State because they deserved to win. So much for my great moment."

Five days later was the big rematch with Michigan, this time in Bloomington. Practices were brutal after the Penn State near-miss. The Hoosiers, who were now ranked No. 1 in the nation, knew they would get Michigan's best shot, especially after beating them early in such a close game at Ann Arbor.

They did, of course. IU won, but only 93-92 in another

IU Archives P-0056038

Bob Knight gives a little smile while walking back to the bench. The 1993 group was Knight's last great team at Indiana.

150

game for the ages. Much like the first meeting, it was a battle from the get-go. Indiana went on a wild 28-8 second-half run, erasing a 70-61 deficit to get ahead 89-78 late. No. 4-ranked Michigan would rally late behind Chris Webber, but would come up short. A Webber three-pointer at the buzzer made for the one-point margin.

With the win IU was 11-0 in the conference and had a three-game lead over Michigan, dashing almost all hope for the Wolverines to win a title with their "Fab Five."

Evans had another huge game for the Hoosiers, scoring 17 points. Cheaney and Nover had 20 each, which had come to be expected. The 17 from Evans was a nice boost. The freshman was starting to become a big piece of this very loaded team.

"Evans played a great game. He stepped up and made some big shots," Cheaney said at the time.

Even Knight had a great summary for where Evans stood. Knight loved his "basketball personality" and his confidence, especially for a freshman trying to find his way on a team loaded with established stars and leaders.

"I don't think Evans has much of a problem believing in himself," Knight said at the time. "He's a little bit deceptive, kind of like he's camouflaged out there. You look at him and you're not sure he's ever shaved. And you say, 'How's this sonofabitch going to hurt us?' "

Michigan coach Steve Fisher was so impressed with Indiana's defense during that 28-8 stretch that turned the game around that he could do nothing but tip his hat.

"We had two turnovers in a row and maybe three or four or five possessions where we were trying to regroup a little bit and get a little confidence and they knocked us down every time," Fisher said at the time. "That run was directly related to their defense."

Indiana beat Illinois again on Feb. 17 to move to 12-0 in

the league and Hoosier Nation braced for another showdown with Purdue, this time on a Sunday afternoon in Bloomington. Another great Robinson vs. Henderson battle was expected in another one-for-the-ages battles between great state rivals.

And then it didn't happen. During practice on the Friday before the game, it changed.

Everything changed.

For the worst. The very worst.

*** *** ***

**It seemed so innocuous** at the time. In a routine drill during a routine practice in a quiet Assembly Hall, Alan Henderson went up to catch a pass during a lay-up drill. And when he came down, his knee buckled beneath him and he went crumpling to the ground.

The non-contact injury was severe. Henderson had torn a ligament in his knee. It ripped the heart right out of him, along with his teammates and coaches.

"When Alan went out, I was just sick for him," former IU assistant coach Dan Dakich said during a 2015 interview. "For us to win a national championship, that really hurt us. But I really hurt for the kid. He worked so hard and was so instrumental to what we were doing. You hated it for him, because he just loved being a part of what we were doing."

It was the same for the players. They knew his serious injury was about to change everything. Their once-complete team, currently ranked No. 1 in the country and blowing through the best league in the country unbeaten, was losing a very important piece.

"When Alan got hurt in practice, that changed everything," Damon Bailey said. "He was a big-time player and at 6-9 he gave us some size inside, but we didn't have much else size-wise when he went out. We had to start mixing and matching quite a bit, and that doesn't always work out the way you want it to."

Henderson, the team's leading rebounder and No. 3 scorer at the time, explained exactly how it happened. "It was just a plain old layup," he said just after the injury. He jumped to catch a pass that was thrown slightly behind him. That was no bid deal; he did it all the time. "Passes aren't perfect. Thousands of times I had made the same move. I was trying to change my direction after I landed, but that wasn't something out of the ordinary. Unfortunately something went wrong that time."

The pain was severe and he knew it was major "because of the way my knee snapped out. I was just hoping it wasn't. The knee injury in basketball that you hear about and do not want to have is a tear in your ACL (anterior cruciate ligament). I was hoping it was cartilage or something, just not the ACL."

The pain the players felt was personal. They hurt for Henderson.

"When I saw it, I wasn't thinking team at all," IU guard Chris Reynolds said back then, a few weeks after the injury. "I was just thinking Alan. I kind of went numb inside. We practiced for about 30 more minutes. It was probably one of the worst practices we've ever had, just because I think inside everybody was just so taken from the tragedy that occurred."

The day before the Purdue game, the torn ACL was confirmed.

IU went out and beat Purdue 93-78 behind Greg Graham's 26-for-28 free throws in their first game without Henderson. Everyone picked up the slack, especially Graham. "They fouled me and I hit them. It's no secret," he said at the time, downplaying his accomplishments.

IU Archives P-0056034

Brian Evans (34) played some critical minutes during his freshman year in 1993, especially later in the year when injuries started to mount for IU.

Despite the victory, IU players were feeling for their friend. Pat Graham called the injury "tragic," but Knight tried to keep them focused on the task at hand. They had to go forward, injuries or no.

"It's just something we have to bounce back from," Greg Graham said at the time. "Like Coach said, our uniforms don't say Alan Henderson or Calbert Cheaney or Bob Knight. They say Indiana. What we had to do was come together, come a little closer, and each player has to step up another level."

Bailey said in 2015 that everyone did a great job immediately afterward of stepping up and doing whatever it took in Henderson's absence. Bailey even guarded Glenn Robinson a lot in the Purdue win, even though he was giving up more than five inches.

"We had enough good players where we could get through it," Bailey said. "We played with a lot of emotion and helped each other out whenever we could. That was just the kind of group we had. We were all in it together, every single one of us."

But Henderson's absence caught up with them two night later when they traveled to Columbus and lost to Ohio State 81-77 in overtime. It would turn out to be their only loss in the Big Ten season, finishing 17-1.

"And the one loss at Ohio State, they weren't that great, but they were hotter than hell that day," Dakich said. "They couldn't miss."

They were taken down without Henderson and without a healthy Cheaney. Years later he told a story of how sick he was that night in Columbus.

"We went 17-1 and the only game we lost — and I never told anybody this — was because I had a 103-degree temperature," he said during an interview a few years ago. "I had only about 10, 11 points. I shouldn't have even been playing. I had no energy to

IU Archives P-0056004

Greg Graham was always a key player for the Hoosiers, but he really stepped up his game late in the season when Alan Henderson went out with a knee injury, averaging more than 25 points per game.

even get out of the locker room. "

IU would win its final four Big Ten games over Minnesota, Northwestern, Michigan State and Wisconsin to close its magical run, winning those games without Henderson by an average of 22 points per game. Greg Graham was stepping up big-time in Henderson's absence, scoring at a 25-point-per-game clip. Cheaney was his usual spectacular self as well, becoming the Big Ten's all-time leading scorer along the way.

Henderson actually played a few seconds in the final home game against Michigan State that clinched the outright Big Ten championship. He had decided to hold off on surgery to repair the torn ligament and even practiced lightly a bit, with a heavy brace holding the knee together.

It was a nice gesture by Knight, so Henderson could be a part of the Big Ten-clinching team. Winning that title mattered, especially after the disaster at Purdue a year earlier had cost them the '92 crown.

"(Winning the Big Ten) is great for us, because we had a lot of disappointing moments. I think back to last year when we had the chance to win it outright and just totally gave it away," Greg Graham said at the time. "This one is really important, because it's our first outright championship, without sharing it with anybody. It's really special. Speaking for my teammates, I think it's one we're going to remember for a long time."

Henderson's departure coincided with the return of Pat Graham from his foot surgery for the Purdue game. He had some big moments down the stretch as well. He remembered those trying times back then, when Henderson went down.

"I saw his knee buckle. As soon as it happened, I turned to go get a drink, because I thought I was going to get sick," said Graham, who had been through multiple surgeries – and rehabs –

157

himself. "When you see a kid go down, even if it's from another team, it just makes you sick because you know how long a road it is, how many bike rides and trips to the weight room you're going to have to make on your own without anybody around to help you and root you on."

It was about to be NCAA tournament time, and the injury led to a lot of reflection from everyone.

``It really hurts when it's someone like Alan, and the team we have,'' Pat Graham said at the time. "With me coming back, I thought we had a better chance to play well. But that's the way things are. And that's just the way we're going to have to play."

# Chapter 10

The NCAA tournament started close to home. The impressive Hoosiers were a No. 1 seed in the Midwest region and got to play in their home away from home in Indianapolis, the RCA Dome. Hoosier Nation loved them and scooped up most of the ticket. More than 25,000 people showed up just to watch practice the day before the tournament started.

The first win was easy. They started their tournament run with a 97-54 victory over Wright State. Senior forward Calbert Cheaney, who had just been named the national player of the year, led the way with 29 points. The Hoosiers also got a few minutes out of Alan Henderson, which was a surprise.

Henderson had torn his ACL in practice on Feb. 19 and no one expected him to play the rest of the season. But after much consultation with doctors, trainers, his parents and coaches, Henderson decided to delay surgery and do whatever he could to help his teammates. He wore a heavy brace on his knee for support and returned to practice in a very limited role.

``There would be times when I would make a move and I would tell myself, `Hey, maybe I will be able to get out there and give us some quality minutes,' ''Henderson said at the time. "I thought if I got in, I could just gut it out and be able to do something."

Henderson played eight minutes and scored four points and grabbed three rebounds. "Every day I feel a little better, and I get a little more confidence in my knee every time out," he told reporters that weekend.

But it would get harder for the Hoosiers, and right quick. Cheaney scored 23 in a difficult test with Xavier and IU hung on for a 73-70 win in front of more than 37,000 crimson-clad fans at the RCA Dome. Xavier had plenty of size inside and the Musketeers kept banging the ball inside all night. Henderson got more minutes but was ineffective and didn't score.

"Quickness is one of my assets," Henderson told reporters at the time. "When they put another big man on me I usually feel I

Brian Evans gets off a pass before Michigan guard Jalen Rose closes in. The Hoosiers played two memorable game with UM in '93, winning both.

can outquick him to get a rebound, or when he's trying to post up, or to beat him down the court. Not being able to do that took a lot away. I wasn't much of a factor."

Still, it was another weekend of two victories.

They were still in the hunt, one of just 16 teams remaining. It was off to St. Louis for the regional semifinals.

Next up was Louisville, a well-coached team by Denny Crum that was loaded with talent. Every game was win or go home and Cheaney was totally focused. He put his team on his back and made sure the Hoosiers advanced. He touched the ball on practically every second-half possession, scoring or assisting on every point in a late seven-minute stretch. IU won 82-69.

"We just couldn't stop him," Louisville coach Denny Crum said at the time. "That's what great players do. They elevate their play and elevate the players around him. Calbert Cheaney took the game over and that was it. We held our own with most of their other players, but it that one stretch he just took the game over. He scored about every time he touched it."

It was win No. 31 for the Hoosiers, and it felt good.

And then there eight.

\*\*\*   \*\*\*   \*\*\*

**But then it** was over. Just like that.

The Hoosiers knew that matchup with Kansas in the regional final was going to be tough. The Jayhawks were very good, and they also had a ton of size. With Henderson injured, everyone could see the matchups were going to be a problem. Kansas had beaten Indiana in December with Henderson and their size wore down IU then.

Replacing Henderson with wing men in the regional final

likely wasn't going to be the answer. Matt Nover was the only big man available and Kansas had two starters 6-foot-10 or bigger, and two more thick big men that came off the bench. Over time, they simple wore out the Hoosiers.

"Kansas was big and we had no one left down there after Alan got hurt," said Dan Dakich, an assistant coach to Bob Knight at the time. "When you see the bracket and you look to see who you need to beat to get to the Final Four, we knew Kansas would be a problem because they were so big.

"Brian Evans did all he could, but he was giving up so much size. And Alan, he tried. He held off surgery and tried to go. But his leg was a mess. He gave it a try, but it just wasn't going to work."

Kansas would win 83-77. They extended their defense to put additional pressure on Cheaney. They also brought in fresh defenders every few minutes to make it even tougher. Indiana got with four now and then in the second half, but couldn't get over the hump. Cheaney had 22, Greg Graham added 23 and Brian Evans added 10 off the bench.

The Jayhawks sent a wave of defenders after Cheaney. Big strong guys, one after another, with their only responsibility being making it tough on Cheaney at every turn.

"Every time I came down the floor and came off any type of screen, they had somebody waiting for me," Cheaney said at the time. "It got frustrating at times, but you just have to fight through it. They extended the passing lane and didn't let us reverse the ball. They just did a marvelous job."

Kansas coach Roy Williams was pleased that IU shot only 46 percent on the night, and only 33 percent from the three-point line.

"We were just trying to wear him down and get him to

162

shoot a lower percentage," Williams said that night. ``We didn't want him shooting 10-for-12 like he did (against Louisville two nights earlier). We've had a couple of other guys we've had to chase around like that, but I don't think any of them were as good as Calbert Cheaney. To me, he is a heck of a player and a great kid."

Henderson could only go three minutes. He tried, Knight tried, everyone tried. But as soon as he got out on the floor, he knew it wasn't going to work. You can play on an unstable knee, even as much as your heart wants you to.

"To Coach Knight's credit, he was never fully confident in putting Alan out there," Dakich said in a 2015 interview. "He didn't want to make it worse. He really cared about that kid. His mom and dad were all for it and Alan wanted to try. He actually did some good things out there in a few of the games, but he was so limited. It was a perfect storm with Kansas because they just fight you in the post so much. It probably wasn't right having him out there."

There was very little to say afterward other than giving Kansas its props. They played better and deserved to win that day.

Still, it was painful that it had to end for these seniors, especially Cheaney. IU coach Bob Knight loved coaching that group, and he hated to see it end.

"The season was great for our kids,'" Knight said at the time. "They did a great job. The seniors, I'm incredibly pleased to have had a chance to have coached these kids. It was a great thing to be able to have them here with us. I think they have left a real impression on Indiana basketball. They put a season together that we can really look back and try to get other teams to match."

The Hoosiers would finish 31-4 but come up short of their goal. Without Henderson, they simply didn't have enough.

IU Archives P-0020240

Alan Henderson recovered from his right knee injury to have two more productive seasons, but he played with a knee brace when the 1993-94 season started. He led the Hoosiers in rebounding all four years.

164

With him? It would have been different. Sure, you still have to win the games but to a man, the Hoosiers felt like they were the best team in the country that year before Henderson got hurt. And more than two decades later, that hasn't changed.

"I have no doubt we were the best team that year," Bailey said in 2015. "Our margin of victory was like 17-point-something and we went 17-1 in the Big Ten in a year when the conference was just loaded with great teams and great players. What we were doing that year was comparable to what the '75 and '76 teams were doing, we were that dominant.

"It just didn't end the way we wanted it to."

\*\*\*      \*\*\*      \*\*\*

**What hurt the most** about that IU team not winning it all was because of the players involved. Calbert Cheaney will always be on any Indiana Mount Rushmore; he was that good. Henderson and Damon Bailey were beloved, then and now. Same with the Grahams, and Brian Evans.

It was such a great, great group of kids. Sure, they were talented, but they were also excellent people. They did Indiana proud. It's still stunning that more than 20 years later that five players on that team – Cheaney, Henderson, Bailey, Greg Graham, and Evans – are still in the top 13 of all-time leading scorers.

They have a special place in the hearts of Hoosier Nation. Especially Cheaney. Everyone loved him, especially his team-mates.

A few years ago, IU guard Chris Reynolds gushed on Cheaney. He said he never met anyone who ever worked as hard as the IU superstar. "He brought his "A" game to every single game. But, more importantly, he practiced extremely hard every single day. What you saw in the game was a result of a lot of hard work. He was constantly thinking about how he could get better. And he could shoot it, too, and that helps."

Henderson shared a similar story a few years ago, as well.

"When we had Calbert here, he was working harder than everybody else, I'd look at him and say, 'Man, he's our best player and he's working that hard. I have no business slacking. I'm not nearly as good as he is,' " Henderson said in an interview with Bloomington reporters. "I had a lot of respect for him. He was just a great person, and a great player. When you see that type of player putting forth the type of effort he put forth in practice . . . I know. I was matched up against him in one-on-one drills and things like that. Coming out of high school, you're not used to having someone score on you. You think whoever you've got to guard, 'Fine, I can stop him.' But I remember calling home and saying, `Mom, Dad, I'm playing as hard as I can and Calbert Cheaney scores on me. Every time.' "

Even two decades later, Cheaney (2,613 points) is Indiana's and the Big Ten's all-time leading scorer. He had a great NBA career as well and now is an assistant coach on Jim Crews' staff at St. Louis.

"For all the Indiana players who have rings, it's a shame he doesn't have one," Dakich said. "He was that good. And you're not going to find a better person. He was an absolute pleasure to coach."

*** *** ***

**H**enderson left IU with quite a legacy too. He's sixth all-time in scoring, first in rebounds, second in blocked shots. And we'll always wonder what might have been.

"I really think, in the history of Indiana basketball, that a lot of people didn't understand how good Alan really was," Dakich said. "He could do everything in the post, he could guard people and he was smart. And let me tell you this. He was a great teammate. He made everyone around him better and we really missed him when he was gone."

They certainly missed him when he couldn't contribute in the tournament in 1993 either. For Bailey, it was always a huge regret to not at least have a chance with a full roster.

"We were just playing so well and worked so well together when we were all there," Bailey said. "We had been together for so long that we always knew where everyone else was going to be. And when Alan went down, we just didn't have a way to replace everything he could do down in the post.

"The worst part was watching Alan try to still be a part of it. I mean, he had a torn ACL and he was still out there with us, practicing when he could and trying to play. For all we know now about ACL's, it was amazing that he could at least try to help us. He wanted to play so bad."

There was one other hard part to watch about the end of the 1993 season. With Henderson out, IU simply didn't have enough size upfront to compete for a title.

Watching the '93 title game made it all even harder when North Carolina won the title. Their star big man was Eric Montross, a 7-footer from Lawrence North High School in Indianapolis. He spurned Knight and Indiana to go to UNC.

He certainly, without question, would have made a difference in an Indiana uniform. Knight's recruiting had started to decline, and Montross was the poster boy for that.

It would only get worse.

\*\*\*   \*\*\*   \*\*\*

The other mark that the 1993 team left behind was that they were Bob Knight's last great team at Indiana. The '94 team still anchored by Bailey, Evans and a healthy Henderson went 21-9 and won two NCAA tournament games before being upset by Boston College in the regional semifinals.

But then the Hoosiers started to drift away from the national spotlight. From 1995 through 2000, the Hoosiers lost 67 games in six years. They had double-digit losses every year except for Knight's final season in 1999-2000, where they finished 20-9. They won no Big Ten titles during that time, no Big Ten tournament titles and were just 2-6 in the NCAA tournament, losing in the first round four times and in the second round twice.

Because the downturn was so pronounced, IU fans often just relied on their memories of recent greatness. That was the '93

IU Archives P-0039748

The 1992-93 Indiana Hoosiers provided a lot of great memories, including a mad dash through the tough Big Ten, going 17-1 on the year.

group, and they provided plenty of wonderful memories.

They had two chances to win, and came up short. But their greatness will never be forgotten. It was a special group of players. They worked their tails off not for individual accolades, but the win a national championship. This was a group of players singularly focused on hanging a sixth banner in Assembly Hall.

It didn't happen, but not for trying.

"You go to Indiana to win national championships and put banners in the rafters," Cheaney said. "We fell short of that goal and the frustrating thing is that I think we had a couple of teams that could have gotten that done."

When Cheaney looks back on his career, he's never one to reflect on a certain shot or a certain game or a certain big win.

To him, his time at Indiana was all about the people.

"The real thing that stands out for me was the camaraderie I had with my teammates on and off the court," Cheaney said. "The most important thing for me was that I had great teammates, and not only just great teammates but great friends in general that I was lucky enough to play with."

And Hoosier fans were lucky enough to watch. It was an incredible two-year run.

**PhotoShop Created Image**
The 2002 Indiana Hoosiers were the first team in the post-Bob Knight era to make a serious run in the NCAA Tournament.

# Chapter 11

**Indiana's magical run** to the 2002 national championship game almost never had a chance to get off the ground.

Nineteen months before Indiana played Maryland for the 2002 national championship in Atlanta, the Indiana basketball program was in a complete state of flux and on the verge of imploding.

Bob Knight – The General – had been fired by the university on Sept. 10, 2000. The final incident that led to his dismissal occurred on Sept. 7 when Knight grabbed a student named Kent Harvey by the arm and reprimanded him after the young man had spoken disrespectfully to Knight in front of Assembly Hall. The incident was reported and three days later IU president Myles Brand claimed the behavior had violated the "zero tolerance" policy that Knight had been working under since the previous spring.

Indiana had 12 players on its roster at the time of Knight's firing and that group was fighting mad. The day Knight was let go, several players made it clear they were considering transferring. The players held meetings together and tried to determine the best course of action. Ultimately, they asked for a late-evening meeting with IU athletic director Clarence Doninger, where they laid out their concerns and set forth their demands for what would have to happen for IU to be able to field a team when the 2000-01 basketball season was set to open in two months.

George Leach, a sophomore center at the time, said the players were unified in their position.

"If things work out the way we want it, we'll stay,'" Leach

told The Associated Press at the time. "We are ready to go if they don't meet our demands. Indiana will not have a team."

Were they bluffing? Maybe. But it wasn't a chance the IU administration was willing to take. A meeting was set for that evening in Doninger's office, where the players stood in solidarity seeking answers.

Kyle Hornsby, at the time a sophomore guard from Anacoco, La., remembers the meeting being intense.

"There were a lot of emotions," Hornsby said. "Some were very calm and well balanced. There were some folks in the room that gave valid points from both sides of the table. There were some very emotional folks, too, who were borderline disrespectful. I was in the crowd of just wanting to hear what everybody had to say."

One of the frustrating things for Hornsby when he looks back on that time 15 years later is that he still doesn't feel like there was anywhere close to full disclosure.

"They weren't going to give us all the facts," Hornsby said in a 2015 interview. "I probably still don't know all the facts. I bet very few people really know all the facts. So it makes it very difficult even now to deliver judgement on who was right and who was wrong. What I do know is that no one was right.

"I'm a little bitter that we weren't able to finish our playing career with Coach Knight. And that bitterness is not directed toward one side or another. It's not directed, for instance, toward just the administration versus coach Knight. It's directed at both. Everybody played a part in this, in what came to be. And so everybody has to take on a little bit of that burden, whether they want to or not."

The critical point for the players was the desire for Doninger to bring back assistants John Treloar and Mike Davis to serve as co-coaches. Doninger complied and ultimately Treloar offered to let Davis be the head coach and he would be the assistant. Back in their minor-league Continental Basketball Association days together, Treloar had been the head coach and Davis had been his assistant. Treloar believed it was time for Davis to be a head coach.

At least that was the conventional wisdom. Looking back, Treloar may have wanted to sidestep the spotlight and under-the-microscope existence that was going to exist for Davis – or any coach, for that matter – in the role of taking the place of Knight, a college basketball icon who had strolled the Indiana sidelines for 29 years and won three national championships. But from a public relations standpoint, it certainly looked like a nice gesture on the part of Treloar.

One of the most outspoken players was Dane Fife, who had said at the time he would leave if IU didn't hire either Treloar or Davis as the interim coach.

"In that moment, it just felt bad," Fife said. "Most of us had come there with a dream of playing for Coach Knight and that dream was being taken away. It just didn't feel right."

But would the players really have walked? Looking back, few believe they would have really carried out that plan but in that moment no one was willing to wait to see if the players blinked.

Ken Bikoff, longtime IU beat writer for both Inside Indiana and Peegs.com, believed the demands were "an idle threat."

"Given the timing of the firing, where were these kids going to go?" Bikoff said. "School had started, and they wouldn't have been able to easily transfer anywhere. Some would have gone, but not many. It's one thing to say you're going to do it. It's a much different issue to actually pull the trigger on transferring. The administration just wanted to get everyone to calm down as quickly as possible, and either Mike or John were the obvious answers to reach that outcome."

Greg Rakestraw, a longtime radio guy in the Indianapolis market, agreed that the timing of Knight's firing in mid-September almost assured the fact that IU would hire a current staff member to get it through the season. He added that when Davis got the Hoosiers to the NCAA tournament his first year, it made it much more difficult to open up the process and hire a new coach.

"Add to that the fact everyone in the administration – and every member of the media – was so glad to be rid of dealing with Knight on a regular basis and felt they were dealing with an actual human being,"Rakestraw said. "That alone was going to buy Mike Davis a lot more time as long as his teams were competent and competitive, which they were at the start."

Reggie Hayes, lead sports columnist for the Fort Wayne

IU Archives P-0022366

Indiana's A.J. Moye, an Atlanta native, stretches out before one of the Hoosiers' NCAA Tournament games.

174

News-Sentinel, doubted if many players would have walked. But even he admitted there was still a possibility with a couple of them.

"Perhaps a headstrong player like Dane Fife or A.J. Moye might have done so if he was totally at odds with the replacement," Hayes said. "But if Mike (Davis) or John (Treloar) had endorsed another coach, that would probably have been good enough to satisfy the players. Mike was the easiest choice to calm the players, however, and I do think that was a key part of the decision. At that point, there would have been few coaches available and willing to take the job on an interim basis even though people talked about Digger Phelps or someone stepping in temporarily. Mike was the right choice for the moment with the exact personality needed."

\*\*\*  \*\*\*  \*\*\*

**The decision to bring** the two coaches back on an interim basis for one season was enough to pacify the majority of the players. Eleven of the 12 decided to stay. Only junior Tom Geyer from Indianapolis, who had scored a total of 21 points in 19 games played in his first two seasons at IU, said he could not stay with a clear conscience. He had come to Indiana specifically to play for Knight and couldn't see himself playing for anyone else.

The reality is there were a lot of players thinking the same thing. The majority, however, believed the right decision was to stay together and try to honor Knight by finishing what they had started.

Tom Coverdale, a 6-2 sophomore guard from Noblesville, Ind. and the 1998 Indiana Mr. Basketball, said the decision the players faced was pretty black and white. Either you were going leave, sit out another year and then have eligibility remaining at another Division I school or you were going to stay and try to make the best of a difficult situation.

"We could have all left and separated but we didn't," Coverdale said in a 2015 interview. "Instead we sort of bonded together and I think that's really what made us such a close team. I think that's also why a lot of us stay in touch even today. You just never know what to expect but when we got hit with that situation we just seemed to come closer together as a group."

IU deputy director of athletics Scott Dolson said it was a difficult time for the program but once the players all got on board they seemed to become a pretty cohesive unit very quickly.

"It was a really good group of players and I think that helped them a lot," Dolson said. "I think they really grew as a team during that whole experience. I also think that's why everyone really rallied around them, too."

Jarrad Odle was a 6-foot-8 forward from Swayzee, Ind. preparing to play his junior season for the Hoosiers. Odle admitted that many of his teammates gave serious consideration to leaving. He said his own decision to stay, more than anything else, was rooted in a value that his parents had instilled in him: commitment.

"I didn't sign a scholarship for Coach Knight, I signed a scholarship that said I was going to play at Indiana," Odle said. "For me it was committing to that program and knowing that if I put my time in, we were going to be successful. And most important for me was that I knew my professional basketball career was going to be very short, if at all, but I knew that I wanted to be an Indiana alum. I knew that later in life, if I needed a job, I wanted somebody out there to be looking out for me. My ultimate goal was to be an Indiana University basketball player and I couldn't be happier to know that I made that commitment to graduate even through some very, very tough times."

For some players, however, it wasn't as easy to just jump

on board. In the fall of 2000, A.J. Moye was a 6-3 freshman guard from Atlanta, Ga. He said the only reason he attended Indiana was to play for Bob Knight. He said he committed to Knight before having ever stepped on the Bloomington campus because he felt a kindred spirit with the IU coach. He also said he still believes today that if Knight had remained the IU coach, that his group of players would have won at least one and maybe two more national championships.

"The thing about Coach Knight was that he loved it like I loved it," Moye said. "I had coaches who called and talked to me and they talked about getting me cars. I had coaches who told me they were going to get me a job or get me some money. I had coaches telling me I could go to their school and I could do this and I could do that.

"But Coach Knight said, 'If you come here, I'm not promising you anything. But if you work hard and you work like you're supposed to work, I can promise you this. We will have a shot at the national championship every year. He said, 'How does that sound to you?' And I said, 'Where do I sign?' "

Jared Jeffries was another freshman on that team, having picked the Hoosiers and Knight over a final two schools that also included Duke.

"Coach told me that he had never had the opportunity to coach a player like me at Indiana and that always meant a lot because there had been a lot of great players come through there," Jeffries said. "That's one of the most disappointing things about never getting the chance to play for him. But there's no doubt that thinking that I had a chance to hang another banner there and believing what Coach Knight said had a big role in my decision to go to Indiana."

Fife, a 6-4 junior guard, had played two years for Knight

177

**IU Archives P-0022336**

Tom Coverdale came to Indiana to play for Coach Bob Knight but really flourished once Knight was replaced by Mike Davis.

178

and always seemed like the kind of kid who fit the Knight mold. Fife's dad was a high school basketball coach back in Clarkston, Mich. and Dane simply had the look and the feel of someone who could have survived four years in the Knight system. That may be a big reason why he has had his own success as a college coach. As of 2015, Fife was an assistant coach on Tom Izzo's staff at Michigan State.

Fife said no one will question why that group of players had chosen to attend Indiana. That much was a slam dunk. But he said there was an affinity toward Davis as well.

"There's certainly no question why Kyle Hornsby, Tom Coverdale, Jared Jeffries, A.J. Moye, Jarrad Odle and guys like that came to play at Indiana," Fife said. "There's zero question. We came to play for Coach Knight. Period. That's it. But the way we saw it was Coach Davis was an extension of Coach Knight. It was pretty simple. And when Coach Knight left the program, we stated that we wanted to win for him and that was true and we did.

"But I thought Coach Davis took a splintered group of guys and got them playing together, and along with some maturity, was able to put us in position that helped us have a chance to be very successful."

*** *** ***

**Indiana would go** 21-13 in the 2000-01 season, finish fourth in the Big Ten with a 10-6 record and make it to the NCAA Tournament, where the Hoosiers were upset in the first round by Kent State. Along the way, Indiana had knocked off No. 1 Michigan State in Assembly Hall on a buzzer-beating shot by Kirk Haston.

Dolson said that was the first moment where he believed

179

Indiana fans started to think everything was going to be all right.

"When Haston hit that shot and we beat Michigan State, I think a lot of alumni started to say that Indiana basketball was going to be just fine," said Dolson, who at the time worked with the IU Varsity Club. "That was the beginning and then obviously what was to come in 2002 just took things to a different level."

Following the 2000-01 season, Davis had the interim tag removed from his title. That led to the 2001-02 season where the Hoosiers went on an unexpected ride that nearly resulted in the Hoosiers hanging that elusive sixth national championship banner.

Derek Schultz, who co-hosts the same radio talk show in Indianapolis with Jake Query, didn't agree with the idea of lifting the interim tag. He was fine with Davis being an interim coach for one season, but he thought it should have ended there.

"The biggest mistake they ever made was not opening that job up," Schultz said. "Detractors say that no one would have wanted to follow in Knight's shadow, but think about where the program still was 15 years ago compared to right now. I don't know if anyone would argue with a straight face that the program's prestige is as high now as it was then. I believe there would've been many high-profile candidates who would have been interested. I like Mike Davis the person – he handled some impossible circumstances about as well as he could – but he should've never been more than the interim coach."

There was also a chasm that existed within the IU fan base. Ultimately, fans were forced to decide if they had truly been IU basketball fans or Bob Knight fans all those years. Those that remained Knight's biggest supporters definitely had a strong feeling as to why Indiana was able to go on that 2002 run. It was quite simple in their minds: Davis had simply taken advantage of the system and had almost won a national title with Knight's players.

The other camp, however, had a different way of thinking. They looked at Knight's final six seasons at Indiana and saw six teams that would make it to the NCAA Tournament but none that would get beyond the first weekend. The feeling was that Knight's teams toward the end of his run at Indiana would simply run out of gas when they got to the NCAA Tournament.

Kit Klingelhoffer, a former IU media relations director and later an associate athletic director, said he never believed the notion that Davis won with Knight's players.

"One thing that team did was get better throughout the course of the season," Klingelhoffer said, "and that was something that wasn't happening in Knight's last six or seven years."

Reggie Hayes, the columnist from Fort Wayne, also said he could see both sides of the argument.

"Part of the statement is true," Hayes said. "You have to consider those players the head coach's players. But Davis had been in on the recruiting of a number of them, so it wasn't like he was taking over players that he didn't already have relationships with. Also, Knight hadn't been able to spur strong postseason play during the years leading up to that. Davis won by being the right type of person to put the players at ease and allow them to play in a relaxed manner during the transition period."

Dave Furst, the sports anchor at WRTV-Channel 6 in Indianapolis, said that IU team may have been Knight's players but they won doing it the Davis way.

"I will never forget a conversation I had with Mike about the motion offense," Furst said. "I explained that kids in Indiana grew up learning the motion offense. Everyone played it. Called it a birthright. But, Mike told me, 'I don't understand it.' I stopped and looked at him, somewhat stunned. 'What do you mean, Mike?' And he said, 'I don't understand the motion offense. I don't get it.'

Jared Jeffries grew up in Bloomington and longed for the day where he could play at IU for Bob Knight. It never happened.

Mike had to put his personal touch on that team and do it his way. And it told me, the Knight era had truly ended."

Radio host Derek Schultz also scoffed at the notion that Davis was winning with Knight's players.

"That is completely ridiculous," Schultz said. "If we want to get technical, Urban Meyer won his first national title with Ron Zook's players. Charlie Weis won with Ty Willingham's players (2005) after Willingham won with Bob Davie's players (2002). I've never bought into the 'winning with another coach's players' assertion. Davis' system was perfect for that specific team – a legitimate lottery pick (Jeffries) surrounded by guys who could shoot the lights out."

Ken Bikoff, longtime IU beat writer for both Inside Indiana and Peegs.com, also never gave much credence to the idea of Davis winning with Knight's players. In fact, he said that notion was just plain wrong.

"There were 11 scholarship players on the 2001-02 team. Six of them, including A.J. Moye, George Leach and Jared Jeffries, never so much as had a practice run by Knight," Bikoff said. "Three more guys – Jeff Newton, Kyle Hornsby and Tom Coverdale – only had one year with Knight. So if nine of the 11 players had either never even practiced with Knight or only had one year with him, is that really Knight's team? And who recruited the bulk of the players? It wasn't Bob Knight. Only two players on that Final Four team – Dane Fife and Jarrad Odle – had any meaningful time under Knight.

"By the time the ball was tipped in the title game, everyone but Fife and Odle had more time under Davis than they did under Knight."

It's a debate that has been waged over the years. But what do the players think? Do they believe that it was as simple as Davis just throwing out the ball and letting "Knight's players" do their thing or do they think Davis was responsible for leading that IU team to the Final Four and beyond?

Moye is in the Knight camp on this one, too. He said with Knight it was all about building a system with all of the right pieces that fit.

"The man was a genius and I learned so much from him just talking to him before I came to Indiana," Moye said. "I never actually got to play for him, which is one of my life's biggest disappointments. But he was the architect of what would end up being the 2002 team that should have won a national championship.

"But did we get to the title game with Coach Knight's players? Of course we did. I mean who else's players were they?"

Jeffries, however, said he didn't believe that way of thinking was fair – or accurate.

"I think it was the system more than the coach," Jeffries said. "You never know what our team would have looked like if Coach Knight had been coaching us. Coach Knight wasn't very high on Dane, Coach Knight wasn't very high on Coverdale. Maybe they wouldn't have even played. I think Coach Davis did a great job getting all of those guys confidence.

Kyle Hornsby said he understands how some people can claim that it was Knight's players that ultimately made the run to the national championship game happen, but just as quickly he said he's not certain how people can justify why that hadn't happened in recent years with some good IU teams, too.

"You can take it the other way and say that coach Knight had good players for the last five to seven years and wasn't able to take anyone even to the Sweet Sixteen," Hornsby said. "So why do you think all of a sudden that he was going to be able to take a team to the Final Four?"

Hornsby said IU did have one player in particular that was someone he described as a unique talent: Jared Jeffries.

"But those other teams had A.J. Guyton who was a unique talent," Hornsby said. "I just think there were a lot of different factors that played into the ultimate success of that team."

Hornsby isn't convinced that IU would have had the same success under Knight. At the same time, he throws out that perhaps the Hoosiers would have had more success. Maybe they would have even hung that elusive banner.

"But we don't know that," Hornsby said. "Maybe we would have had less. Maybe people would have left, maybe people would have transferred. People could have gotten burned out. I saw that happen with a couple of players that played under Coach Knight. So you don't know how things would have played out. So for people to go out on a limb and say one guy did it for this reason is just pure speculation."

Fife has the utmost respect for all the things Knight was able to do in his Indiana career but he takes issue with those who think the 2002 season was Davis winning with Knight's players. Fife said who is to say that some of IU's key players from that season would have even found the court under Knight?

"The bottom line is you're trying to get a group of guys to play together, to win basketball games. In our case, it was Coach Davis and Coach Treloar putting us in the right position," Fife said. "I don't know if Coverdale would have played under Coach Knight. I really don't. I don't think anybody thinks he would have. Andre Owens left that team before the season. Kirk Haston went pro. So a lot had to be done to get that team playing together.

"Yes, we committed to play for Coach Knight but I think ultimately Coach Davis was able to carry on when Coach Knight had left and make some changes and make us better. I think it was our way of honoring Coach Knight, embracing Coach Davis and winning for Indiana."

Coverdale has difficultly with the concept that he wouldn't have been able to play in Knight's system. He said he has heard it all before and he simply doesn't put any stock in it. People point to the fact that in his only year with Knight, Coverdale played less than 40 minutes total all season and scored 10 points.

Don Fischer, IU's radio play-by-play voice, had been with Knight throughout his IU years though and doesn't believe Coverdale would have played under IU's legendary and often stubborn head coach.

"I don't know if Knight ever told (Coverdale) or not, but

Mike Davis always had to fight the argument that he won at Indiana wih Bob Knight's players, but he considered them Indiana players, not his.

basically I don't think he thought he was good enough after he got there," Fischer said. "And that's the thing about Knight. If he saw something in a guy that he didn't like and he didn't feel like he could get it out of him, he didn't waste the time. And I think he saw a number of things about Coverdale that he didn't like."

But Fischer is also quick to point out that Coverdale wasn't about to let that deter him either.

"He just kept fighting to play," Fischer said. "And then when Mike (Davis) took over, it was like a new lease on life for him. Mike gave him the opportunity and he took advantage of it. Tom Coverdale was just a tough guy, in fact maybe one of the toughest guys I've ever seen play at Indiana."

While Coverdale insists he could have played in Knight's system, he's a firm believer that 2002 happened because of the subtle changes that Davis made with the personnel that had been assembled.

"I don't think you can say it's someone else's team when the head coach is there and dealing with every situation that a team goes through on a day-to-day basis," Coverdale said. "He is the one that is managing different personalities, and our team chemistry was so good and Coach Davis had a lot to do with that."

***   ***   ***

**And what about** Davis himself? He was asked the question during a 2015 interview, a decade and a half after he took the reins of the IU program. He said to his way of thinking there was a common denominator that stood out above everything else with the players that played for him that first season at Indiana.

"When I hear that, I say it's fine because they were all Indiana players," Davis said. "We won basketball games because we had a really good team. That much I know. Jared Jeffries would demand the double team. We had guys like Odle and Fife and Hornsby and Coverdale who could all really shoot the basketball. We had Jeff Newton who was skilled and is the all-time shot blocker in school history for a career. We just had a group of guys who knew their roles and played those roles really well."

But was it Knight's players, or was it your system that ultimately led to the turnaround?

"The whole time I was there, it was just more of a distraction about Coach Knight getting fired than anything else," Davis said. "It wasn't about Indiana basketball, which should have been the primary focus. I believe once our guys were able to block things out and just play basketball, that's when we showed everyone that we were a pretty good basketball team."

# Chapter 12

When the Indiana basketball team reached the Big Ten portion of its season in 2002, there was really no reason to believe that in a few months the Hoosiers would be playing for a national championship.

In fact, sitting at 7-5 and coming off a 66-64 loss to Butler at Conseco Fieldhouse just four days before the conference opener, IU had a different set of worries on its mind. They just wanted to find a way to qualify for the NCAA Tournament.

The Butler game was on a Saturday and that Sunday, the day before New Year's Eve, the IU team hung out together in Bloomington. Tom Coverdale remembers having a long conversation with Jarrad Odle about what the next few months might hold for this Hoosier basketball team.

"At that point, Indiana had made it to 16 NCAA tournaments in a row and we were just talking about how we can't be the team that didn't make the tournament and broke that streak," Coverdale said. "That's what a lot of people were talking about at that point. I think we had a lot of guys that had some fear of failure in them, which I think sometimes can be a good thing. That fear just seemed to push everybody to a different level."

In the 12 games leading up to the Big Ten, Indiana had played up-and-down basketball. The Hoosiers had played in the Great Alaska Shootout early that season where it dropped a 50-49 decision to a Marquette team led by Dwyane Wade and coached by Tom Crean. Five days later, IU won a road game at North Carolina.

The next time out, the Hoosiers went on the road to Southern Illinois and lost by 12. That was followed by a home win over Notre Dame.

Up and down. Up and down. That was the theme of the 2001-02 Indiana Hoosiers.

Jared Jeffries said losing to Butler just before the Big Ten hurt, but it was nothing like the punch in the gut the Hoosiers experienced when they lost at Southern Illinois.

"I don't think people understand that when you go into a gym like that and it says Indiana across your chest, you just can't afford to lose. It's not acceptable," Jeffries said. "In games like that, teams are sitting there waiting on you and that's their biggest game of the year. And they had a good team. They had some guys on their team from Indianapolis and they definitely had a chip on their shoulder because they weren't recruited by Indiana.

"And they played well and deserved to win. But we came out of there looking at each other and just wondering 'What's next?'"

Kyle Hornsby said after the Butler game there were a lot of guys on that team who were a little more than concerned.

"We were looking around at each other and thinking 'Man, this could get bad,' " Hornsby said. "And maybe things had to truly hit rock bottom before everyone could come together and accept their roles."

After the Butler loss, the third defeat in four games for IU, the Hoosiers were 7-5 heading to the Big Ten. If the panic button hadn't been pushed at this point, it was very close.

"You always want to say that we were supremely confident at that point in the season but I think the reality is most of us felt like we were in trouble," Jeffries said. "We were a very low confidence team at that point and we were scrambling for answers."

IU coach Mike Davis said what he remembered most about

that non-conference season was simply the level of opponents that Indiana had played in preparation of what they would face in the Big Ten.  In 12 pre-conference games, IU had played seven teams that would go to make the NCAA Tournament field that year: Charlotte, Marquette, Texas, Southern Illinois, Notre Dame, Miami and Kentucky. Two other teams – Ball State and Butler – had been ranked in the top 25 when the Hoosiers played them. One of the other games IU had played was a road game at North Carolina. It was far from the cupcake schedules that IU would often play in future seasons.

"When I look back on it, a lot of the high-level teams today play really weak, almost non-competitive nonconference schedules and I just remember that it seemed like every team we played was really good," Davis said. "That Southern Illinois team went to the NCAA Tournament as an 11 seed and beat Texas Tech and Georgia to get to the Sweet Sixteen.

"So what I was focused on was more of the competition we had played than anything else. We never had a break with that schedule. We didn't have those six or seven games to make our record look good. I was just happy to get to the conference, to be honest. In some ways, I was more comfortable playing conference teams."

IU radio voice Don Fischer said he felt like it was a team with promise that hadn't figured out how to play together just yet.

"The thing I remember about that team was that I just felt like they had underachieved at the point in the season," Fischer said. "They hadn't found themselves, so to speak. They weren't playing up to their capabilities."

Fischer said it reminded him a lot of the 1981 Hoosiers that went on to win the national championship. In '81, Indiana was also 7-5 going into the Big Ten.

**IU Archives P-0022381**

Indiana guard and Noblesville native Tom Coverdale drives around an Oklahoma defender during the 2002 Final Four in Atlanta. Coverdale battled an ankle injury during the postseason, which slowed him down.

"I wasn't thinking at that point that this was a team that could duplicate the feat of the '81 team, but I was thinking this was a team that had a lot of talent and if they could just find a way to put it all together, they had a chance to be pretty good," Fischer said.

*** *** ***

**One of the interesting** themes with the 2002 Hoosiers was how IU had to recover from three significant sprained ankle injuries over the course of the season. Everyone remembers the one suffered by Coverdale in the NCAA Tournament and the way that became a media circus all its own at the Final Four in Atlanta.

Another sprained ankle was suffered by Jeffries in a mid-Big Ten non-conference game against Louisville on Feb. 9. Because of it, Jeffries wasn't able to play in a disheartening 64-63 home to Wisconsin a few days later, a game that IU players point to as being a big reason why IU didn't win the Big Ten title outright.

But perhaps the biggest sprained ankle of them all came on Jan. 2 in the opening tip of the Big Ten opener at Northwestern. IU center George Leach came down awkwardly and rolled his ankle and didn't return.

That cleared the way, however, for Odle to enter the lineup. From that point forward, he become one of IU's most valuable players. Odle would start 23 of the final 24 games. He ended up the third-leading scorer on the team behind Jeffries and Coverdale, averaging 8.8 points per game. He was also third in rebounding, with five boards per game.

Before Leach got hurt, Odle was not destined to be an IU player that anyone remembered. But when IU fans look back on the 2002 season, they can't do so without thinking about Odle's contributions.

"I thought Odle really took us to another level," Davis said. "When you look at it, we had three guards who could really shoot the basketball but when we inserted Odle into the lineup when George got hurt it just gave us one more really good shooter in there because Jarrad Odle could really shoot the basketball, too. He wasn't really a 3-pointer shooter but he was right there on that line. Just inside of 3-point range, Odle really felt comfortable and that gave us a completely different look.

"He was a tough guy, who had a lot of pride and he could really shoot the basketball."

Odle said the lesson he learned was that even when things aren't going well, you need to prepare yourself to be ready if an opportunity ever presents itself. Looking back, he believes he was more than ready when Davis looked down the bench a few seconds into the Northwestern game and called his name.

"My three and a half years leading up to that point, I was an arrogant college basketball player that thought I should have been playing more minutes whether I really should have been or not," Odle said. "I think some of that, with that little chip on my shoulder thought. 'Well here it is, and I'm going to take it and I'm going to run with it.' Basically I never wanted to give Coach Davis a reason why he could take me out of the lineup. And I continued to play pretty well and I played my role. I didn't try to be anything that I wasn't. I knew who our stars were and the guys who were going to score a lot of points and I just tried to do everything else to help us win."

Jeffries called Odle's insertion into the lineup IU's "turning point of the season."

"I hated to see George go down because he had a put

194

together a pretty good summer and he was working real hard for us," Jeffries said. "But that was obviously the turning point of our season. Once Odle got in the starting lineup, I think everything clicked. I think he gave us the basketball IQ and the spacing that we needed in our starting group."

Dane Fife said that Odle was simply the missing link that IU needed at that point in the season.

"What we had with Jarrad was a guy we could depend on," Fife said. "He wasn't going to do anything to beat us. He gave us a bulk inside that we needed, where Jeffries and Newton and Leach gave us contrasting styles. Odle was the physical presence that we needed. He started playing a lot better. Coach Davis did a great job of helping Jarrad understand what he was good at, what were his limitations and Jarrad played his role very, very well."

With Odle producing in the starting lineup, the Hoosiers had more balance. The starting group included a three-guard set of Fife, Coverdale and Kyle Hornsby with Odle and Jeffries in the front court. IU also had good depth with A.J. Moye and Donald Perry at the guard positions and players like Leach and Newton coming off the bench to give frontcourt support.

One of the things that made the 2002 IU team special was that, for the most part, it was a group of role players that all executed those jobs well. Jeffries was the one star, but everyone else simply contributed.

"We all knew in the locker room that Jared Jeffries was our superstar," Odle said. "Cov was a role player. Hornsby was a role player. We all had our different attributes. But at the end of the day, when you put all of those together, we were all able to play those roles. Some nights some guys would step up and play out of their skin a little. My game was against Louisville when I had 25. But we had other guys who stepped up on nights when we needed

**IU Archives P-0022382**

Indiana coach Mike Davis is all smiles as his Hoosiers make a run during the NCAA Tournament. Davis replaced Bob Knight in 2000.

196

someone to step up. Sometimes they just did the little things but everyone handled their role incredibly well."

That new IU lineup quickly was able to get the Hoosiers on a roll. IU opened Big Ten play with four consecutive wins including top 25 victories at home against No. 25 Michigan State and on the road at No. 13 Iowa. After a road loss at Ohio State, the Hoosiers won three more in a row to open conference play at 7-1.

Included in those three victories was an impressive 88-57 home victory over an Illinois team that came into the game ranked No. 9 in the nation. The Hoosiers led by 11 at half and opened the second half on a 26-6 run. Everything was clicking from the perimeter and IU hit 17 three-pointers, which at the time was both a school and Big Ten record. Fife hit 6 of 7 from beyond the arc and finished with a game-high 20 points.

At 7-1, IU was in the driver's seat to win the Big Ten. But the up-and-down tendencies that had plagued the Hoosiers in the non-conference season returned in the second half of the Big Ten. Over the next seven games, IU would go 3-4. The previously mentioned loss at home to Wisconsin with Jeffries sitting on the bench with an ankle injury was particularly hard to handle.

The final two losses of that stretch – at Michigan State and at Illinois – appeared to have the Hoosiers on the outside looking in to have any chance at earning a share of a Big Ten title.

But on the same day that IU lost on the road to the Illini, the Hoosiers received a big boost when Michigan State went into Columbus and upset the Buckeyes. Suddenly, all the Hoosiers had to do was beat Northwestern at home to claim a share of the Big Ten title for the first time in nine seasons.

Odle was sick on the bus ride to Illinois. How sick? So sick that he couldn't eat anything when the team stopped at the Beef House, a popular IU stop off of I-74 in Covington, Ind. near

197

the Indiana/Illinois border. He still played in the game but on the first time down the court hurt his back and didn't play well.

Odle said the team was down after losing to the Illini and feeling like it had ruined any chance it could have at getting a co-Big Ten title. This was before social media where you could find out instantly the result of a game such as Michigan State-Ohio State. The Hoosiers didn't hear about it until they returned home to Bloomington.

"That was long before the age of Twitter and Facebook and all of that stuff, so we didn't really get the news until we watched ESPN SportsCenter," Odle said. "Even though we wanted to be outright Big Ten champs that year, there's still a Big Ten championship banner hanging in Assembly Hall with our year on it because we played well enough in the games that we needed to in order to make that happen."

Hornsby remembered it a little differently. He thought the team found out as it was boarding the bus to head home from Champaign, Ill.

"I remember almost being in tears at realizing that not only was that Illinois game within our grasp but if that had been anywhere else but Illinois we would have won that game," Hornsby said. "We had already lost at home to Wisconsin which had taken away our chance to control our own destiny and now losing to Illinois we thought we may have just lost our chances at a share of the Big Ten title and that was devastating.

"So to hear that Michigan State had pulled one out at Ohio State, I think everyone was elated that we still had a chance to seal the deal with Northwestern at home."

IU beat Northwestern 79-67 in the Big Ten regular season finale as Tom Coverdale had 20 points and five assists. Jared Jeffries was named the Big Ten MVP and Dane Fife was honored as the conference's co-defensive player of the year.

The Hoosiers then went to the Big Ten Tournament where they beat Michigan State 67-56 to avenge a road loss from two weeks earlier. The next day IU lost to Iowa on a 15-footer at the buzzer by former IU player and 1997 Indiana Mr. Basketball Luke Recker.

If you ask a couple of people from the 2002 team about that shot – including IU head coach Mike Davis – you'll learn that there's a conspiracy theory involving Recker's shot that day. Some claim that replays showed there was a clock malfunction and that actually the shot shouldn't have counted.

"Go back and look at the tape," said A.J. Moye. "Something happened to that clock. The clock was running and then it held at 4.6 or something or 3.2 or 2.2. The clock just stopped there for a full second and then it kept going. If that clock didn't have that glitch or someone hadn't of pressed that button the shot wouldn't even have counted. I'm telling you. If you go back and look at the tape, that's the crazy thing about it all. That was a good shot, but it didn't count."

Davis said the same thing.

"They've made changes now to how the clocks run because back then there were times when you'd go back and look and the clock would freeze for a second or two," Davis said. "That's something that got fixed but the reality is that shot should have never counted."

\*\*\*     \*\*\*     \*\*\*

**All that remained** for the Hoosiers now was the NCAA tournament.

"I kind of had the same philosophy as Coach Knight

always had and that was I never worried about the Big Ten Tournament too much," Odle said. "We always wanted to play well and we wanted to advance but I'm not completely convinced that playing three or four games in a row doesn't kind of take you out of sync in getting ready for the tournament.

"So for us, it put us in a tough position with a loss where we have to go back and we have a day or two to recover before we figure out where we're going. I think we were all upset that we lost but at the end of the day we all had a bigger goal in mind. I think we were looking forward to seeing where our next season would begin."

When Jared Jeffries saw Indiana's name appear on the television screen on Selection Sunday headed to Sacramento to play the University of Utah, he wasn't thinking about the fact that

IU Archives P-0022405
Indiana made it to the Final Four in Atlanta in 2002 and it was the first time in 10 years that the Hoosiers had reached the big event.

IU was about to play one of the game's most colorful and respected coaches in Rick Majerus.

He wasn't thinking that if somehow IU could get past the Utes, they would likely play a University of Southern California team that was stacked with talent and had at least four future pros.

He wasn't thinking that if IU could get to the Sweet Sixteen, the game would be played in Rupp Arena in Lexington, Ky.

No, as he perused the bracket in the South Region of the 2002 NCAA Tournament, Jeffries' eyes always locked in on one name: No. 1 Duke. For the Hoosiers to advance in the NCAA tournament, they would have to somehow do the unthinkable and upset the top-ranked team in the country.

"It was a difficult draw for us because you were thinking even if you found a way to get out of Sacramento you didn't really want to play Duke," said Jeffries, who actually chose Indiana over Duke in his final college selection process coming out of high school. "They were probably the best team in the tournament. They had five or six pros on that team. And we hadn't matched up well all year with good, quick guards and Jay Williams was the national player of the year."

Jarrad Odle had a completely different train of thought when he looked at that same bracket. For him, it was more of a personal thing. His mother had had some health issues and hadn't been able to travel to many of the longer road trips that year. There was no way she would be able to make it to Sacramento for the first two rounds and selfishly Odle really wanted his mom to be there when he capped off his college basketball career. He knew she could make it to Lexington.

"So my goal was to No. 1 make the Sweet Sixteen but No. 2, I knew we would be back in Lexington where my mother could at least see me play potentially my last college game on the court,"

Odle said.

Long tournament runs weren't the norm for IU then. Far from it. IU hadn't played in a Sweet Sixteen since 1994. So the last seven seasons prior to 2002, the Hoosiers had made seven NCAA Tournament appearances but five times had lost in the first game and the other two in the second game.

"It did not take long for people to come to terms with the fact that we had not made it out of the first round of the tournament in a long, long time," Hornsby said. "So we knew we had to beat Utah first and foremost. Myself, I had lost to Pepperdine and Kent State and I was sick of that.

"We just wanted to get past the first round and then deal with whatever came next."

Before, IU could think about the Sweet Sixteen, however, the Hoosiers had to focus on the round of 64. First up was a Utah team that was 8-0 all-time in first-round matchups under Majerus. The Utes were the No. 12 seed facing No. 5 Indiana, but a lot of people were predicting a potential 12-5 upset.

Davis wasn't seeing what all the experts were seeing, though. He believed that Utah would have a difficult time adjusting to how well IU could shoot the ball and also how well his team was executing.

"Our offense was really quick at that time," Davis said. "We moved the ball and we shared the ball and it was like a machine. When we played Utah it was really kind of funny because we just whooped them all over the court. We made shots, we were making crisp passes and we were really just starting to come together and gel like the team we always thought we could be."

Indiana raced to a 42-27 halftime lead but in the final minute before the half the Hoosier faithful held their collective breath as Tom Coverdale was down on the ground in a heap, clutching his ankle. He had the ankle taped and returned in the second half. He finished with 19 points, eight rebounds and four assists in IU's 75-56 victory.

Looking back, 13 years later, Coverdale remembered the play as if it were yesterday.

"It was the end of the first half against Utah and I jumped up off a fast break to make a pass and I just landed on it wrong and that kind of started it," Coverdale said. "It was never completely good after that but I did my best to play through it."

A.J. Moye said that right from the start in the NCAA tournament, beginning with Utah, he started to get the feeling that there was no way Indiana was going to lose.

"I think we came out in that first game against Utah, and I think it was a little battle but then we just hit a gear with Jared and Newt and they were dominating inside," Moye said. "And we just kept moving the ball, moving the ball, moving the ball."

Moye was particularly impressed with the way Jeffries took control.

"He really was like a maestro to the whole offense," Moye said. "Jared Jeffries is one of the most cerebral players that I've ever been around. Talking and communicating, that's the player I learned that from. He would talk and communicate to everyone. Defensively, he'd be in the back and he'd say 'There's a flare screen on your right' or 'Pin down on your left' or 'Switch, switch, switch, get out, get out, get out.' I think it was just a thing where we were all focused."

Don Fischer remembers that Utah game well, and that Majerus was complimentary of Davis for the game plan he had installed.

Fischer had a friend named Jimmy Edwards who lived in California and was a good friend of Majerus. That night, after

203

IU Archives P-0022373

Indiana's Jarrad Odle battles for the ball in the paint during the Hoosiers' national champiionship game with Maryland. Indiana started to turn its season around once Odle took on a more prominent role.

204

the game, Edwards invited Fischer to a dinner with about 20 other people that Majerus attended. This was just an hour or two after Utah had been eliminated by Indiana.

"Obviously Rick wasn't in a very jovial mood or acting in his usual fashion but what he said was how he was so impressed with the coaching job that Mike (Davis) had done," Fischer said. "My friend told me later that Majerus went back and looked at that tape and plotted all of the sets that Mike had used in that game and then Utah used those sets the next year.

"It was the ultimate compliment."

Indiana's first big break of the NCAA Tournament came following the win over Utah. The No. 13 seed, UNC Wilmington, knocked off USC in overtime, 93-89. Suddenly, all that was standing in between IU and a trip to the Sweet Sixteen was a No. 13 seed.

"Going through a tournament like that you have to have some breaks and that was definitely one of ours," Coverdale said. "USC getting beat with a big strong team and having a great year and then getting to play Wilmington was definitely a break. Not that they weren't a great team but it was one that we felt like we were better and more talented than."

Fife said the challenge after Wilmington beat USC was not looking past the Seahawks to a potential game with Duke. Wilmington had a big scorer named Brian Blizzard and he torched the Hoosiers for 27 points. With 2:45 to play, the Seahawks rallied to within three at 66-63. But it was too much Jeffries for the Hoosiers down the stretch as IU closed the game on a 10-4 run to post a 76-67 victory. Jeffries had 22 points and seven boards to lead the Hoosiers.

"We didn't play well against Wilmington but we got by them," Fife said. "We were pretty excited that they beat USC. I just remember that Blizzard gave me 27 or something like that. I just remember that I spent the whole game in foul trouble but I think Jeffries might have been the MVP of the region. Jared Jeffries was playing like the first rounder that he was."

Kyle Hornsby said one of the reasons Blizzard went off against IU was that Fife got into early foul trouble.

"If Fife didn't get in foul trouble, then I wouldn't have had to have been the next to guard him," Hornsby said with a smile. "I just remember they stuck me on him and that guy was really good."

Davis was feeling like IU had really hit its stride and was playing it best basketball of the season. You always want to peak at the right time and have a little extra left in your tank when you get to the NCAA Tournament and Davis believed his team had just that.

"Wilmington was a good basketball team but we were playing at that point like a team that wasn't going to be denied," Davis said. "Our perimeter guys were making shots and a guy like Jeffries was making all the plays around the basket. It just gave us a team at that point that was becoming very hard to defend."

# Chapter 13

**M**ention the **2002** Indiana basketball season to a die-hard Indiana basketball fan and ask them to name one game and 99 out of 100 people will say the same thing.

Duke.

The Duke Blue Devils were the No. 1 team in the nation and the No. 1 overall seed in the 2002 NCAA Tournament when they squared off with fifth-seeded Indiana in the Sweet Sixteen at Rupp Arena in Lexington.

The week of the Duke game there was a flurry of media activity in Bloomington as everyone wanted to talk to the up-and-coming Hoosiers. Most, it seemed, believed this was a good story but one that needed to be done quickly because IU would not survive another game in the tournament.

It was that kind of sentiment that really ate at A.J. Moye.

And so he spouted off in very A.J. Moye-like fashion, which, meant Moye could have said just about anything. He was always the most colorful, most unpredictable quote in the locker room. Prior to his sophomore season in 2002, Moye responded with an answer to a reporter's question and used the names Charles Manson, Jeffrey Dahmer and Mahatma Gandhi all within a two-sentence reply.

The question: How do you think your team is going to fare this season?

This was a guy who once said he was so deep in Mike Davis's doghouse that he was having his mail delivered there. He said he had had cable installed.

No, this was A.J. Moye quote extraordinaire being told by

the national media that the Hoosiers had no chance against Duke. And this was a player who not only absolutely hated to lose but in this case, thought his team was pretty good, too.

And so early that week, Moye went off.

His most famous quote: "It's not like they're the University of Jesus Christ and we're playing the Twelve Disciples. It's just Duke. Duke is just a name on a jersey."

Another Moye quip: "They put their basketball shorts on the same way as I do, one leg at a time."

The coaches weren't quite as amused. The last thing they wanted that week was bulletin board material for the Blue Devils. The reality, though, is that Moye's comments may have taken some of the focus off of Indiana as a team and on to the 6-3 guard from Atlanta.

"Whatever I could do to help," Moye said many years later with a smile.

But again, that was simply Moye.

"I just remember that whole week before and everybody was counting us out," Moye said. "Everybody was saying something. And they weren't even interviewing me. And I just got pissed. And that's when I said what I said. And I remember coach and the media relations people telling me, 'You can't speak to the media anymore.' It was funny but it was true. And I remember when I said that thinking, 'Well we've got to go out and prove it now.' "

Moye didn't understand why everyone expected Duke to blow the Hoosiers out of the building. Yes, Duke was 31-3 and had a lineup of future pros. Indiana was just 22-11.

One thing Moye never lacked was confidence, IU coach Mike Davis said. Sometimes that confidence would get him in trouble, but more often than not he was able to back it up.

"I remember he was the same way when we recruited him," Davis said. "Moye was always the most confident guy in the room. But he could back it up, too. Moye was a really good teammate."

IU's Dane Fife credited Davis and John Treloar with creating the perfect atmosphere back in Bloomington the week before the Duke game.

"They kept that week as normal as possible," Fife said. "I think the whole state of Indiana was in a frenzy. But our coaches kept our locker room and our team, as a whole, focused. They kept the hype down for us. They helped us remember that 'Guys, this is what we're supposed to do.' This is Indiana, let's keep this in mind. We're Indiana. We're not a Cinderella."

The game itself was one that was difficult to comprehend. Duke came out hot and led by 13 at halftime. At that point, IU had committed 16 turnovers that had led to 23 Duke points.

"I told them at halftime that I thought we had them right where we wanted them and some guys looked at me in disbelief, but I just felt like we had figured out what they were trying to do and now we needed to go out and execute," Davis said. "They weren't leaving our shooters. (Mike Krzyzewski) was a really smart coach and everyone else that we had played throughout the year had worried so much about Jared Jeffries posting up that they would double-team him and triple-team him.

"That kind of threw us off in the first half because when Jared would get the ball he was always looking for someone to pass it to. And Duke was not leaving our shooters, so it was a different look."

In the second half, IU focused on getting the ball inside and the game changed.

"Once we started figuring it out, we made layup after layup

**IU Archives P-0022341**

IU coach Mike Davis pushed all the right buttons during the Hoosiers' run through the 2002 NCAA Tournament.

and got the ball going to the basket. Our game plan and our style of play had been taken away but when that didn't work I thought our big guys did a good job of taking over the game."

IU hung around in the second half thanks to a flurry of shots by Odle in the paint but the turnovers continued to mount. With 12 minutes to play, Duke led by 14 at 59-45.

And then the Hoosiers just willed themselves to victory. It was as if IU was not going to be denied.

Those final 12 minutes will go down as some of the most exhilarating in Indiana basketball history. Davis had told his team before the game that to play basketball at Indiana was a great honor. And then he said, "If you do something special, the fans of Indiana will remember you for the rest of your life."

The 2002 Hoosiers did something special.

IU climbed back in the game with a combination of favorable bounces, a ton of made free throws, some big defensive plays and one big shot after another.

One of the most memorable plays down the stretch was when the 6-foot-3 Moye went up from a standing position underneath the basket and blocked straight down the shot of 6-foot-9 Carlos Boozer. The play resulted in a jump ball and Rupp Arena was as electric as it had been the entire game.

At the very least, it was a huge momentum swing for the Hoosiers.

"I know I surprised Boozer on the block," Moye said. "He's going up for the dunk. He's thinking 'I'm just going to dunk this.' I know I surprised him. I know I surprised a lot of people. People don't really realize it, but I can get up. I can get up. I still can. I probably still hear about that block two or three times a week and that was 13 years ago."

There were a few other big plays at the end of the game

that almost didn't go nearly as well for the Hoosiers. IU had taken a 74-70 lead with 11.1 seconds to play following a pair of free throws by Moye. It looked like Indiana was going to win.

"I thought we had the game won," Davis said. "And then a few seconds later, after they got an offensive rebound off a missed free throw I thought we were going to lose. It was the craziest final 10 seconds of a game that I can ever remember.

"I remember that it seemed like that last 10 seconds took about two hours."

Duke came down and missed a three-pointer but the ball got kicked back out to Jay Williams and he launched another three-pointer. He made it and was fouled with 4.4 seconds to play. The television commentator on the game said the foul had been on Jeff Newton. Don Fischer, on the IU radio network, initially said the foul had been on Tom Coverdale.

Both were wrong. Dane Fife was the culprit. Whether he actually fouled him or not is up for debate but the truth is he got too close in that situation than he should have been.

Williams then had a free throw to tie but he missed – and Boozer got the rebound.

Boozer went back up for a shot to give Duke the win but Jeffries deflected it and Newton got the rebound and IU had won 74-73.

Fife maintains to this day that he didn't foul Williams. But then again, Fife only admits to about three or fouls total in his four-year IU career.

But he said the following week that had Duke found a way to come back and win that game that he would have never returned to the state of Indiana. He would simply withdraw from school and never show his face in Assembly Hall again.

A bit dramatic? Sure. But if IU had squandered a four-point lead against the top team in the nation in the final five seconds it would have gone down as the most memorable collapse in IU history.

Fife can joke about it now.

"I think they would have had my picture at the borders and all the ports of entry and wouldn't have allowed me back in the state," Fife said. "But I think it was all divine intervention. Coach Knight always said that God doesn't care about who wins or loses, but I don't think so that night. I think it was all part of history. It was divine intervention to make that game special. You couldn't have a finish where a game just simply ends. It had to be an exciting finish."

Just talking about it though gets Fife mad all over again.

"That definitely wasn't a foul," Fife said in a 2015 interview. "The problem was that pride got in the way. I felt like I had done a pretty good job in the second half on Jay Williams and I wasn't about to give him a free shot, an uncontested free shot at that. Let me just say this about that shot. If the person is competitive, no one in their right mind would have allowed Jay Williams to get a free shot."

But while that is the play most people will talk about in that game, perhaps even the bigger play happened after Williams missed the free throw. Somehow, Boozer got to the offensive rebound and had a chance to win the game for the Blue Devils but was unsuccessful on the put-back.

Many people say that Jeffries fouled Boozer and the officials swallowed their whistles. Hornsby said while that may be true, Boozer wasn't completely innocent on the play himself.

"Boozer fouled him," Hornsby said. "He fouled him. And if you aren't going to call the first foul, you can't call the second. If you watch the replay, it looks like Boozer just cleaned him out

213

of the way. But really what did he have to lose at that point? If he doesn't get the rebound the game is going to be over. But when I've watched that replay over the years, I just thought Boozer shoved J.J. out of the way.

"And it wasn't close."

And what about Jeffries? Did he think he fouled Boozer at the end when the Duke big man had been able to snag that offensive rebound?

"Oh yeah," Jeffries said, flashing an ear to ear grin. "You always foul late in a game like that. Ninety percent of the time the refs don't want to decide a game at the end like that."

Davis said he has never watched the replay of the Indiana-Duke game. Never. He said living it once was enough.

"It was just too nerve-wracking," Davis said. "I remember

IU Archives P-0022376

Indiana guard Dane Fife (center) raises his hand to celebrate a Hoosiers' victory during their dramatic NCAA Tournament run.

thinking we had won it, and then came the Fife foul and I thought, 'We're going overtime' and then Jeffries misses the block out and I think 'We're going to lose.' And then Jeffries probably fouls him and they didn't call it and we were off to play the next game."

Davis's quote in the newspapers the next day was a simple message: "We shocked the world."

"And we did," Davis said. "No one thought we were going to beat Duke. They were the No. 1 team in the nation and their roster was filled with future NBA guys. They had a loaded team. And there was no way anyone would have picked us to win. But our guys never quit, they kept playing through everything and in the end, they continued playing basketball."

$$*** \quad *** \quad ***$$

**O**nce the Hoosiers started on their roll, there was no turning back. Dave Furst, the sports anchor for WRTV-Channel 6 in Indianapolis, said he remembers how much Davis was enjoying the moment.

"The momentum grew with each win and Mike Davis was riding it," Furst said. "I never saw him turn down an interview request. The media ate it up. Don Fischer ate it up. For the most part, IU fans everywhere did, too. Given the circumstances, I remember calling it a cathartic experience for everyone who ever wore a shirt with an IU logo on it."

One of the great moments from the celebration that ensued inside of Rupp Arena in Lexington the night that Indiana knocked off Duke was to see former IU basketball player turned radio color commentator Todd Leary standing on his chair courtside with his arms in the air celebrating the moment.

"I got a little carried away," Leary would say later. "It was a great moment for a great team and I just got caught up in the moment."

Don Fischer refers to that game as one of the greatest he had ever called in his 40-plus years as the Indiana play-by-play voice. But he does admit that when he saw Leary on the chair he was a bit taken back.

"I was stunned," Fischer said. "But with Todd, it was such a legitimate excitement. It wasn't like he was playing a game or acting like a fool to get attention, he was totally emotionally elated. In some ways people thought it was very unprofessional, but to me it more of what a moment this was for him. He was just so thrilled that this team had accomplished something that no one thought they could accomplish."

*** *** ***

**N**ext up was Kent State, a team that had knocked off Pittsburgh to reach the Elite Eight. If Indiana had played a lot of teams at that point after an emotional win over Duke, it might have suffered a letdown even with a trip to the Final Four on the line.

But IU had a bad taste in its mouth about Kent State. The Golden Flashes had eliminated IU from the NCAA Tournament the year before and for Fife in particular it was even more personal than that. Fife remembered reading a story after the Kent State game the year before where a player on that team, Trevor Huffman, had taken a shot at IU's inability to play good enough defense. Huffman had 20 of his game-high 24 points in the second half of a 77-73 win over IU.

So what did Indiana do in the game to reach the Final Four? The Hoosiers jumped to an early lead, made their first eight three-point shots and finished by hitting 15-of-19 three-pointers overall, a school record for the NCAA Tournament. Fife hit 6-for-7 by himself.

Indiana won 81-69, but Fife said that if Coverdale hadn't reinjured his ankle the Hoosiers would have really won big.

"If Coverdale doesn't get hurt, we win by 25," Fife said. "Cov got hurt and they made a little run to make it interesting at the end. There was just no way that Kent State was coming close to beating us. After that kid was talking trash the year before, this game was over before it started."

It all paid off that night against Kent State and the reward was a trip to the Final Four in Atlanta.

"That night I don't know if there was a team in America that could have beaten us with the way we were shooting," Odle said

Fischer agreed.

"They just seemed to play that game with the basic mentality that if they could beat Duke they could beat anybody," he said. "And on that night, with their confidence and the way they shot the ball, I honestly believe they could have beaten anybody."

*** *** ***

**So it was on to** Atlanta for the Final Four, where the Hoosiers were now just two improbable wins away from hanging a sixth national championship banner in Assembly Hall.

Reggie Hayes, the longtime sports columnist for the Fort Wayne News-Sentinel, said even though IU was clearly the long-shot among the Final Four teams a lot of people were beginning to believe.

**IU Archives P-0022388**

Dane Fife scans the floor as an Oklahoma defender closes in on him during IU's national semifinal game in 2002.

"Once they reached the Final Four, I did wonder if this wasn't just one of those improbable sports stories that seem to crop up from time to time that don't really fit any rational explanation," Hayes said.

After Coverdale got hurt against Kent State, the media circus began leading up to the Final Four. There was a Coverdale Watch ongoing in Bloomington and everyone wanted to know the same thing: Would Coverdale play on Saturday against Oklahoma in the national semifinal game?

Moye still laughs about it today. He said he and his teammates were 100 percent convinced that Coverdale would play against the Sooners.

"I'm telling you this, man," Moye said. "With Coverdale, you would literally have to break his legs for him not to play. We weren't worried if Cov was going to play. We weren't worried that Cov couldn't move. It wasn't like Cov was blazing fast to begin with. Cov was a 'Get you out of position and then drive his shoulders straight through the middle of your chest' type of player. All you had to do was hesitate just a little and Cov was gone.

"But we all had complete faith in Cov. I knew it was bad but Cov was like 'It's cool. I'm gonna play.'"

Playing the Final Four in Atlanta was big for players like Moye and Jeff Newton in particular. They were from Atlanta and getting to that Final Four was truly the culmination of a dream.

"When we found out the Final Four was in Atlanta, me and Newt said we were going to work our butts off to go to the Final Four," Moye said. "That summer after my freshman year, we worked like maniacs. And after that, every summer we would do that. But that summer of 2001, we really put in the work. And it was really cool that we were able to see that all pay off. And then to see Newt have that great game against Oklahoma, really did my heart well."

Davis was surprised at the lack of respect Indiana was receiving going into the Final Four. He was hearing all the same things, which was basically that Oklahoma was simply too good. They were going to be able to press and trap IU all over the court and it was going to be tough for IU to even get shots off. Basically, the sentiment nationally was that IU wasn't going to have an answer for several of Oklahoma's players.

Davis remembers being perplexed after he watched film on Oklahoma, wondering what was everyone else seeing that he wasn't.

"I was kind of laughing about it, to be honest," Davis said in a 2015 interview. "Because I wasn't seeing what everyone else was seeing. I didn't think they were going to be all that difficult to play. We could really shoot the basketball and if you were going to put in a trap, that meant that somebody was going to be open for a shot.

"So I just turned the film off and started to focus on who we would play next."

Oklahoma was coached by future IU coach Kelvin Sampson. The Sooners already had beaten teams like Kansas, Maryland, Connecticut and Arizona that season. The Sooners were an overwhelming favorite to win the game.

But three Indiana players in particular really stepped up for the Hoosiers. Two were familiar names – Dane Fife and Jeff Newton. The other, however, was Donald Perry, who filled in when Coverdale couldn't go.

Fife locked down Oklahoma guard Hollis Price, who had just won the MVP of the West Regional, and held him to 1 of 11 shooting and a total of six points. Newton had one of the best games of his career and was dominating inside. He had 19 points and IU won the game 73-64.

As for Perry, the redshirt-freshman guard only played 11 minutes in place of Coverdale but he scored seven of his 10 points in the final three minutes to help the Hoosiers win. Perry averaged 2.6 points per game but came up biggest when his team needed him the most.

"Donald is overlooked in a lot of these stories when people look back on that team," Hornsby said. "He came so far that year. When he showed up, he was a very gifted athlete but he was a turnover machine. In practice, we just abused him. He could barely get the ball into the frontcourt or make a pass to the wing without us picking it off."

Coverdale remembered how well both Newton and Perry stood out for the Hoosiers offensively in that game.

"Newt just picked us up when we needed it, and then also Donald," Coverdale said. "In the second half when I struggled a little bit they took me out and put Donald in and Donald just stepped up and made a couple of great plays. Then he made a great pass to Newton over the top to give us the lead for good. It was like every other game in that tournament when it got into the second half we felt like we were going to win. Just like the whole season, it was different guys stepping up in different games."

\*\*\*     \*\*\*     \*\*\*

**As easy as it was** for members of the 2002 team to go back and watch the replay of that win over Duke, it's hard to watch the championship game against Maryland.

After playing at such a high level for five consecutive NCAA tournament games, the Hoosiers just didn't have it against

**IU Archives P-0022360**

Indiana freshman Jared Jeffries battles for a rebound against Maryland in the national championship game in 2002.

the Terrapins.

In the previous five games, the Hoosiers shot 55 percent from the field against Utah, 56 against Wilmington, 50 against Duke, 64 against Kent State and 52 percent against Oklahoma.

The Hoosiers had been on fire. Against Maryland, IU hit 20 of-58 shots, only 34.5 percent from the field. IU did make 10 three-pointers and that allowed it to hang around for a while but it wasn't enough.

There was also a huge free throw disparity in the game as well. IU made 2 of 7 foul shots while the Terrapins hit 20 of 28.

Somehow, Indiana rallied to take a 44-42 lead with under 10 minutes to play, but Maryland responded with an 11-2 run and recaptured the game's momentum.

Coverdale said he has only watched the Maryland game a few times but never past the point where IU takes its final lead.

"It's just something I can't do," Coverdale said. "Just being that close and then not doing what we had done every other time in that tournament was really frustrating. They just made plays and we didn't. You have to give them credit for that but in the back of your mind you're more frustrated in that was the game that we didn't get it done."

Fife said Maryland did what Indiana had done to that point in the tournament: it found ways to make plays in clutch situations.

"They just had too many horses," Fife said. "They hit big shots when it mattered. They had tremendous size. And size was always our weak spot. With that said, (guard) Juan Dixon was the one that hit the huge shots down the stretch to get Maryland the win. Juan Dixon just hit huge shots."

Jared Jeffries said he hates to admit that another team was better than IU, but he said he feels like Maryland was clearly a much more talented team.

"We played OK but in my opinion the game itself wasn't a great game," Jeffries said. "Both teams were very nervous and didn't shoot the ball well. A lot of mistakes were made. We had a chance to win and we wanted to make that shot and keep that run going but it didn't happen. But we gave ourselves a chance to win that game and win a national championship and that's something that's really important, too."

Some players don't like to even think about the Maryland game. A.J. Moye is one of them. When he looks back on the national championship game, he can feel a knot develop in his stomach.

In five NCAA Tournament games, Moye had been a big contributor off the bench for the Hoosiers. In four of the five games, he had played 15 minutes or more. In the national semifinal against Oklahoma, Moye had played 20 minutes.

Against Maryland, for all the marbles, Moye played only seven minutes, hit his only shot and didn't have a rebound. When Indiana really needed some toughness on the floor, their toughest player was stuck on the bench.

"I'm probably more upset now than I was back then," Moye said. "I guess I'm just wired different that way. But I didn't understand it then and I don't understand it now. I just felt like I didn't get that opportunity. And I know in my heart that I could have done something. It was kind of hard just to watch. But it was like, 'What are we saving me for?' It was the last game of the year."

The coaching staff simply felt it was a matchup issue and went in a different direction from Moye. They also played fewer players than normal. Beyond the starters, Newton played 28 minutes and Perry had 10 to back up Coverdale, but that was it.

"I just remember thinking, 'What the heck?' " Moye said.

"I just didn't feel like I was able to have any effect on the game. I don't understand it. I don't get it. I still don't get it. That's probably why I really don't like to talk about the championship game because it just makes me mad."

Hornsby led IU in scoring with 14 points and Fife was the only other player in double figures with 11. Jeffries had only eight points on 4 of 11 shooting.

Hornsby remembered the game more for the fact that IU didn't have answers on defense more than anything else.

"Their game plan was to get the ball inside and take advantage of us down there," he said. "And they were huge. And unless we were going to be able to score on them down in the post like the way they were scoring on us, it was going to be a very difficult game to win. Not to mention, it was an ugly game. It was just flat-out ugly."

Davis said in the title game it simply wasn't Indiana basketball the way the Hoosiers were used to playing it.

"We played for the championship but we really didn't play for the championship the way we knew we could play," Davis said. "In some ways it just felt like we were more excited to have made it to the championship rather than focusing on winning the championship game. And that's on the coaches, not on the players."

*** *** ***

**H**ow special did this team become for the Hoosier Nation? Ken Bikoff, longtime IU beat writer for both Inside Indiana and Peegs.com, was asked if he had any anecdotes to share about the 2002 Indiana basketball team. He had one in particular that said a lot about the way the '02 Hoosiers touched the Indiana fan base.

"I watched the NCAA title game that year with a friend of

IU Archives P-0022351

Kyle Hornsby fires up a jump shot during the NCAA championship game against Maryland in 2002. Hornsby was the top scorer that night with 14.

mine, another IU alum, and my girlfriend, who is now my wife," Bikoff said. "She was crying in the car on the drive home after the game. I'll never forget what she said: 'Damn you. I never cared about this stuff before I met you.'

"This was a woman who thought I was lying when I said there was an NBA team called the Golden State Warriors, so that's where her sports knowledge was. But that woman, someone who didn't give a rip about sports at all, fell in love with that team and that group of players, and she was crushed when they lost. She has never felt like that about another team to this day.

"No team has ever touched her like that one. That's how special that group was."

**PhotoShop Created Image**

This banner never made it to Assembly Hall, though it could have. Led by Mike Woodson and Isiah Thomas, the 1980 Hoosiers were loaded.

# Chapter 14

**Expectations are ingrained** in the DNA of every Indiana basketball fan. Every year, it's all the same. Not five minutes after one season ends, Hoosier fans begin breaking down the next season, dreaming big dreams, sheltering potential concerns and talking the big talk.

It's how we're wired. We expect good things. Some years, we expect great things.

That's what makes the 1979-80 Indiana Hoosiers somewhat unique. They are one of only three IU teams ever to be ranked preseason No. 1 in the Associated Press poll – the 1976 and 2013 teams are the others – but the 1980 group is often overlooked as one of the greatest teams in IU basketball history.

And that's flat-out wrong.

There was plenty of debate when this book project was being put together about which IU team would be the fifth one we'd highlight as a missing-banner candidate. We considered 1975, 1993, 2002 and 2013 as no-brainers. There was discussion back and forth on the guys from 1954, 1960, 1984, 1992 and others and 1980 wasn't always the first candidate. There were logical reasons for arguments against: No signature nonconference wins, a nondescript Big Ten season outside of the final few weeks, no exciting tournament run. All were valid, but for this one point:

That all *could have happened*.

"They all sure could have happened," said Steve Risley, a rugged junior forward on that 1980 team. "The potential was definitely there. I mean, seriously, look at that roster. Look, Mike

Woodson and Isiah Thomas are two of the greatest players in IU history and we went out there with both of them side by side, feeding off each other's greatness. We had a ton of other weapons, too.

"It's just a shame we couldn't keep it all together for an entire season. We won it all the next year, of course, but much like those '75 and '76 guys talk about, I say the same thing. In my mind, our 1980 team was better than the 1981 team that won it all. We were that good. Well, that good when we were all out there at the same time. That just didn't happen much. Injuries just killed that team, and when they showed up, we didn't really respond very well to picking up the slack."

IU fans were starving for a title chase that season because success had been fleeting for three years after the great run of the 1976 group that featured Scott May, Quinn Buckner, Bobby Wilkerson and others. In their final three years from 1974 to 1976, that group went 86-6, culminating in the '76 unbeaten champions, considered by many as the greatest team in college basketball history.

What followed, probably to be expected in the ebbs and flows of college basketball, was a downward turn. In the next three years, IU went 59-31, didn't win any Big Ten titles and won only one NCAA tournament game from 1977 through 1979. The 31 losses over a three-year period were substantial. Knight didn't lose that much again at IU until the very end of his 29-year career.

There could have been some inside fixes. Knight, who played the redshirt card very well through the years at Indiana and was a bit of a Big Ten innovator in that area, often admitted that had he started redshirting people sooner in his career that the lull might not have happened. He often said that if he had redshirted Tom Abernethy and Jim Crews for a year each during that 1975-76 run, that the 1977 team that only had Kent Benson back would have been much better.

Some great recruiting classes during the Knight era also never panned out. That was the case in 1976, when six recruits arrived to Bloomington, all with great acclaim. Mike Woodson and Butch Carter stuck around for four years and Woodson was an all-time great. But other potential stars like Derek Holcomb, Mike Miday and Bill Cunningham soon transferred. Glen Grunwald, the top high school player in Illinois that year, battled injuries throughout his career and wasn't able to contribute as he and others thought he would.

"Bob (Knight) had a pattern of building a nucleus in one class and then filling in after that," longtime Bloomington Herald-Times sports editor Bob Hammel said recently. "It was that way with the '93 team when you go back to how it was built in 1989 with Cheaney, the two Grahams (Greg and Pat), and the guys that would contribute there. Matt Nover was a year ahead but redshirted and so he was part of that class, too. Then the next year they added Damon (Bailey) and the next year they added Alan (Henderson). But the nucleus was all in that first year.

"And it was the same with the '75 and '76 teams with the Scott May and (Quinn) Buckner and (Bobby) Wilkerson group, and they thought they had the next group in place with Woodson's freshman year, but that one just kind of scattered into the hills and it set everything back for that period a little bit. They needed to regroup and get some things back together."

Woodson was spectacular from the day he arrived on the IU campus, but there were very few other bright spots during those three years, which produced 11-, 8- and 12-loss seasons. Most of what got written on a national basis about Indiana basketball during those three years wasn't pretty.

In fact, it was oftentimes downright ugly.

Mike Woodson had such a quick first step that he could get to the basket against anyone. He left IU as the school's second all-time leading scorer, despite missing nearly two months in 1980 with a back injury.

And that's never good.

*** *** ***

Two events served as ugly precursors to the 1979-80 season. One happened during the summer, when IU coach Bob Knight was coaching the U.S. team at the Pan American Games in San Juan, Puerto Rico. Knight got into an argument with a police officer before a team practice and he was accused of assaulting the officer. Knight got the "Ugly American" tag roped around his neck and Puerto Ricans considered it an insult that Knight basically thumbed his nose at them.

He was convicted of a crime in abstentia and sentenced to six months in jail. It was all wildly blown out of proportion. Knight argued vehemently that the police officer lied about the events, that the cop had actually first poked Knight in the eye, and there were plenty of witnesses who agreed with Knight, including U.S. assistant coach Mike Krzyzewski, the legendary Duke coach who had played for Knight at Army and was coaching there at the time. Krzyzewski always had Knight's back – and rightly so – that Knight was never the instigator in the blow-up.

Still, it was a negative story, but it was really more about Knight than the players, even though Woodson, Thomas and IU's Ray Tolbert were also on that U.S. team. The story dragged on for months. Puerto Rican law officials wanted Knight extradited, which was never going to happen, of course. Knight eventually apologized, but it wasn't roundly accepted by the Puerto Ricans.

The other negative from the previous season ripped right through the IU roster. During a November trip to Alaska for a tournament that included two losses, more than half of the IU players used marijuana. When that information came to light for Knight a

233

week or so later, it tore him apart. In his 2003 biography, he said the event and the subsequent fallout "hit me as hard as anything ever in coaching."

Knight kicked three players – Jim Roberson, Don Cox and Tommy Baker – off the team and put the others, who were considered first-time offenders, on probation. That group included Woodson and Tolbert – "some of the best kids I've ever had. That was very tough to handle," Knight said.

Thirty-five years later, Risley still calls it the most emotional night of his life when the team gathered at Assembly Hall to deal with it all.

It was that tough.

"That night in the locker room, that was the hardest thing I've ever gone through in my life," Risley said. "I wasn't involved in it, and I was grateful I wasn't, but as teammates you hated to see

IU Archives P-0022040
Seniors Butch Carter (left) and Mike Woodson were captains of the 1979-80 Indiana basketball team. Both played and coached in the NBA following their playing careers at IU.

all that happen. I think Knight had gotten tired of Jim Roberson and Don Cox. Cox came from Broad Ripple with Woody, but he wasn't really a good fit with us. It was hard for Tommy Baker. He was a really good player and I think it was tough on Coach to let him go, too.

"It was finals week, and we all just stayed in there for hours. I mean, players were crying, coaches were crying. It was a tough night. The guys who just got probation, they had to call their parents and talk to them. That was the only way they would get to stay. For those guys, Coach left the discipline up to the parents."

The 1979 team would finish 22-12 and in the middle of the pack in the Big Ten. They got an invite to the NIT tournament and made the most of it, beating state-rival Purdue in the finals at Madison Square Garden in New York.

Three games in a year with Purdue. They were going to get used to that.

\*\*\*   \*\*\*   \*\*\*

**That was actually** a very interesting time in the Indiana-Purdue rivalry. It was, at least for two years, very civil. Even though there was a lot at stake in both 1979 and 1980, animosity was at a minimum. Lee Rose was the new coach at Purdue and he stayed just those two years but there were no issues between the two programs, even though it was ugly beforehand and would get very ugly again a year after he left.

"During my entire time at Purdue, I never had a cross word with Knight. Not one," Rose said in a 2015 interview. "When I took the Purdue job, I didn't really know any of the Big Ten coaches. I had heard there had been some problems between the two schools, but when I first saw him at the Big Ten coaches meeting,

IU Archives P-0055972

Ray Tolbert (45) was a dominating presence inside for Indiana all season. He was quick around the basket and an exceptional rebounder, and would battle defensively with all the standout big men in the Big Ten in 1980.

I went up to him and we talked. I said to him 'I don't know about what's gone on before, but you're not going to have any problems with me. And he said to me 'You've just done something no one else has ever done.'

"It was a nice exchange and we never did have a single issue. I respected the heck out of him as a coach and really enjoyed competing against him."

It wasn't much different with the players.

"We all knew each other so well. We had a lot of Indiana kids and so did they," Risley said. "We'd play at Hinkle (Fieldhouse) together all summer at Butler and no one even knew we were all there. There'd be a lot of the NBA guys there too. Magic (Johnson) and (Greg) Kelser would come down and (Larry) Bird was there a lot too.

"Purdue was really good then, and we were, too. We had our battles on the court and it was about as even as it could be during my career. Don't get me wrong, we always wanted to beat the heck out of them, but there was always plenty of respect between the two of us."

The civility even showed with the coaches.

"Any time I ever saw Coach Knight, he was always cordial with me," Purdue's Lee Rose said. "Even later, when I worked with USA Basketball and whenever I saw Coach Knight there when we were picking teams, we always had nice conversations.

"When we played at IU and lost, I congratulated him and his players. And when we won at Purdue, he even came into our locker room and congratulated my kids. It takes two people to do that. There were a lot of strong personalities in the Big Ten, but I didn't have a problem with any of them. Especially Bob Knight."

Winning the NIT in 1979 was a nice way for all the Indiana players and coaches to end a difficult season. There was hope for the future. IU had plenty of great wing players and talent inside with the big guys.

There was only one thing missing. A point guard.

But he was coming.

*** *** ***

**The recruiting of** Isiah Thomas was a national story, even back in those days before the 24/7 recruiting websites. Thomas

IU Archives P-23287

The close bonds between Ray Tolbert (left), Mike Woodson and Isiah Thomas actually started the summer before. They played on the 1979 USA Pan Am Games team that was coached by Bob Knight.

238

was a Chicago legend from the mean streets on the west side of town that were covered with gangs and guns and drugs. He was the youngest of Mary Thomas' nine kids and a superstar in the making. For some, he was the best high school point guard they had ever seen. He had a lot of fans.

Including Bob Knight.

Knight wanted Thomas in the worst way. Thomas was under a lot of pressure to stay home and play at DePaul, the Chicago school that was a national powerhouse back then and had made great inroads in recruiting and keeping Chicago kids. Other Big Ten schools also pushed hard. But Mary Thomas liked that Knight was honest and a disciplinarian, too, just like she was. She knew Indiana would be a good fit for her little boy. The discipline in Knight's program mattered to her.

"That's how my mom raised me," Thomas told the New York Daily News in 2008. "(Knight) was a lot softer on me. She admired his honesty and discipline. At the time, he was one of only a few coaches who didn't come in and try to bribe my mom. My mom never took the money."

It was a perfect fit, right on down to how Knight treated Thomas during his two years in Bloomington.

"What I remember about Coach is how he was yelling at me just like my mother. Every swear word that my mother used, he was using, and I was like, "Have they been talking about me?"

So when Isiah chose Indiana – "it just seems right," he said at the time – Isiah was happy. Mary Thomas was happy. And Bob Knight was very happy.

He had the final piece.

*** *** ***

239

**W**hen they first assembled as a group for the 1979-80 season, the players felt good about chasing a national championship. They had talent at every position, plenty of veteran depth and a great freshman class headlined by Isiah Thomas.

"I definitely thought we were that kind of team, the kind of team that could win it all," Risley said. "We had strong senior and junior classes and we had Isiah coming in. That's why they picked us No. 1. We were all set to make a run at a title."

Thomas, of course, fit right in.

"He was ahead of his time as a young player. He had tremendous talent and skill," junior big man Ray Tolbert said recently. "He had to adjust quickly and buy into Coach Knight's philosophy and his extreme demands, but he caught on very fast."

Sports Illustrated, which was a big deal back then, picked IU to be No. 1. They wanted to come to Bloomington for a photo shoot and story. But Knight, who had several run-ins with Sports Illustrated reporters in the past, refused to cooperate. SI ran a simple cover, with an Indiana jersey with a No. 1 on it, a huge departure from their usual artistic photo covers.

They were ready to go.

"Being ranked No. 1 was a great feeling, but the way Coach Knight saw it was more like a challenge to keep us focused on just playing basketball rather than basking in our newfound success," Tolbert said. "We were looking forward to the challenges of being No. 1, to see if we could match the '76 team."

So was everyone else in the Hoosier Nation.

# Chapter 15

It didn't take long for the country – or the world, for that matter – to figure out how good this Indiana team really was. In preparation for the 1980 Summer Olympics in Moscow, the Soviet Union national team was making a November tour through America, playing exhibition games against a dozen or so of the best college basketball teams around the U.S.

Knight already had taken on Puerto Rico in the summer and everyone wondered how he'd handle the Russians. As a precursor to the Olympics, a first-ever World Top 20 basketball poll was released of the top amateur teams across the globe. The Russian were tied at the top in the rankings, not with the U.S. or any other country, but with *Indiana University*. That's the respect this team got.

Polls never meant much to Knight, and this one didn't either. "I think about it the same way I think about most polls," he said at the time. "I don't think people know what they're talking about this time of year."

But from the opening tip of the game with the Russians, IU earned that respect. They won 78-50 and it wasn't even that close. Mike Woodson led the way with 28 points, Randy Wittman added 12 and the Hoosiers had five players in double figures. They strategically and methodically picked apart the Russian zone, scoring at will.

The Russians' best player, Sergei Belov, had the quote of the night in his very-broken English: "Against zone, move move

move players, move move move ball."

Beating the Russians – a team that would win the 1980 Olympic gold medal the following summer – was a huge confidence boost for Indiana.

"When we first started in 1980, we were a dominant team," IU forward Ted Kitchel said. "We played the Russians, they came over and played us, and we beat them by 20. We knew we were going to be good."

The first three games of the regular season were all romps for the No. 1 Hoosiers. They beat Miami of Ohio 80-52 in the opener, then pounded Xavier 92-66 and UTEP 75-43 to win the Indiana Classic in Bloomington. The only disappointment early was a foot injury to promising freshman forward Steve Bouchie. The 6-8 forward from Washington, Ind., started the opener but then missed three games.

IU Archives P-0055991

Many people questioned if the relationship between flashy point guard Isiah Thomas and hard-headed disciplinarian Bob Knight would work, but they turned out to make each other better. Thomas left IU a champion.

Knight wasn't saying many good things publicly but there were signs of something special brewing. Woodson was scoring well – he had 28, 28, 26 and 32 points in IU's first four outings – and was named tournament MVP. Even his postgame comments, however, spoke of looking at the bigger picture. "This means a lot to me," he said then, "but a national championship will mean a lot more."

The IU guards showed a lot, too. Flashy freshman point guard Isiah Thomas had a great running mate in Randy Wittman, the sophomore who had burst onto the scene a year earlier. They continued to play well in a tight win over No. 16-ranked Georgetown, winning 76-69 against a very good Hoyas team that shot 63 percent from the field and still lost. Thomas led a pressuring defense that forced 19 turnovers and he scored 19 points while Woodson added 23. They were a lethal one-two punch.

But there were also concerns.

\*\*\*    \*\*\*    \*\*\*

**I**njuries were nagging the Hoosiers a bit. Highly thought-of freshman Steve Bouchie – who had been Mr. Basketball in Indiana a year earlier at Washington High School – missed several games after the opener with a foot injury. Wittman had been battling an ankle injury as well and he hobbled onto the floor for the big showdown with No. 5 Kentucky.

It would be Wittman's last game of the season. He would re-injure his ankle in the second half, and never return.

"Wittman going down, that hurt so much," junior forward Steve Risley said. "He and Isiah were great together as guards. They would have been something really special. They're two of the smartest players I ever played with and they really loved playing

243

Randy Wittman (24) was one of Bob Knight's all-time favorite players. He said Wittman made the transition from high school to college better than any freshman he had ever coached. His injury in 1980 was devastating.

together."

Knight always raved about Wittman. He was a standout from the day he got on campus, shining as a freshman in that '79 season. He was so good that Knight said Wittman had "made the best adjustment from high school to college basketball as any freshman I ever coached."

The Hoosiers missed Wittman immediately. They lost 69-58 to Kentucky in Lexington. They were called for four illegal screens in the first half and fell behind. Thomas was in foul trouble throughout and Wittman left for good with his injury just two minutes into the second half. Woodson had a rough day, shooting just 4 of 18 and not scoring at all in the second half, a 20-minute segment where they scored only 19 points as a team.

Something didn't seem right with him.

Indiana beat Toledo in Indianapolis, with Woodson starting at guard alongside Thomas now that Wittman was out. The rotating starting lineups were nothing new. In fact, by season's end, 12 different players would start a game for IU.

Next up was No. 8 North Carolina on Dec. 22 in Bloomington, but the bad news – the very bad news – came a day earlier. That's when IU announced that Woodson would miss the game with what was described as a pinched nerve in his back. It ended a stretch of 96 consecutive games played for Woodson. The Hoosiers lost at home 61-57, and didn't look very good doing it without their leader and best player on the floor.

About the only player Knight was happy with through December was Thomas. The two losses to Kentucky and North Carolina bothered him, of course, but he also wasn't very happy with how people were playing even in the other wins, many of them routs.

"Thomas has been far and away our most consistent

player, which is pleasing but at the same time a little bit distressing from the standpoint that we haven't been getting that consistency from some of the players who have been around two or three years," Knight said at the time.

But the bombshell came the day after Christmas, after tests determined that Woodson had a herniated disc in his back. He underwent surgery in Indianapolis, and his time away from the team was undetermined. It could be a few months, or it could be more. It also could be season-ending. No one at the time really knew for sure.

Knight was devastated. He had seen all the work Woodson put in all summer as part of Knight's Pan American Games team and had seen how much he cared about having a great senior season.

"I have never felt worse for any player for any reason than I do for Mike, because I think more than any person, I know how much he looked forward to his senior year," Knight said at the time.

Woodson averaged 21 points a game in the first six games, but he was never playing at 100 percent. He would wind up missing 15 games, six of which would be Indiana losses.

"We had some things going for us early in my senior year but then again, hey, sometimes things happen in basketball and you have to play throught it," Woodson said a few years ago. "For me, it's the guy that can get up and keep it going."

Woodson would work like crazy to rehab after the surgery. But without him, a once-promising season fell apart quickly. This team just wasn't the same without him. They missed his talents certainly, but they missed his leadership even more.

"When Woody got hurt, it threw us all off. We had a guy or two who didn't play team ball," Risley said. "It was a very cliquey team and without Woody, well, we missed his leadership. We never got to the point where all 12 of us shared the same team goals. It's kind of like racing. It takes everybody on the team to win. We didn't really have that, and it's too bad."

*** *** ***

**W**ith **Woodson and Wittman** gone, Thomas had to take over the team and he was more than capable. He hit a game-winner to beat Tennessee 70-68 right after Woodson's surgery, scoring 20 for the first time in his IU career and surviving a quick benching after committing six turnovers in the first half. He also had magical moments once the Big Ten season started.

"Isiah was such a charismatic person. And when Woody went out, he became our engine," Risley said. "He did a fabulous job on the court. Even though he was a freshman, we never looked at him like that. He was a leader from the beginning.

"Isiah had all these great individual skills, but he was completely a team guy. He was a team-first guy for sure. When we lost Woody, we lost our rock, but Isiah stepped right in. He'd speak up in the locker room all the time, which you just don't see in a freshman. He carried us, that's for sure."

Or tried to. It would take some time for Thomas to adjust to Woodson being gone.

The Big Ten season started with a thud, with a one-point loss at No. 5 Ohio State (59-58) and a 52-50 loss at Wisconsin to quickly fall into an 0-2 hole in the league. Thomas had 15 points against the Buckeyes but had been burned several times gambling too much on defense. Against Wisconsin he shot just 6 of 22, playing all 40 minutes and trying to do too much on his own.

They bounced back with four straight wins, beating Michi-

All three games with Purdue during the 1980 season were very physical, as evidenced by IU freshman guard Isiah Thomas (11) getting clobbered by Purdue's Keith Edmonson on the way to the basket.

gan, Michigan State and No. 13 Iowa at home and Northwestern on the road. Thomas had only six points against the Wolverines, but added eight rebounds and eight assists. He had 19 against Michigan State and started to look a little more comfortable running the show.

Against Iowa he had 14 points and 13 assists and was in constant attack mode. That wasn't all good, because he picked up three charging fouls and had to spend a good bit of time on the bench. But the win at Northwestern was special. Thomas, coming home to Chicago, scored a career-high 28 points. "We knew he was ready tonight," Knight said at the time. "He got off the plane smiling."

They fell to 4-3 in the conference with an ugly loss at Minnesota, scoring a season-low 47 points in a rough 55-47 defeat. Thomas scored only four points on 2 of 4 shooting, once again dealing with foul trouble from the start. He picked up his fourth foul with 13:22 to go in the game and wasn't a factor. It was becoming troubling that this team just wasn't very good offensively if Thomas wasn't at his best. Foul trouble was killing him, and no one else in the backcourt was filling the gap.

IU came home to beat Purdue (69-58) and Illinois (60-54) but then went to Purdue and lost 56-51. Thomas picked up three fouls in the first three minutes and didn't score until only 10 minutes remained in the game. He finished with 12 down the stretch but only played 22 minutes.

"It was a good thing we were playing Isiah as a freshman that year," Purdue coach Lee Rose said recently. "He was a great player, and he was way better the next year. But as a freshman he was so aggressive and always pushing things so hard that it would get him in trouble sometimes. That happened against us in the game at home. He was in big foul trouble almost immediately."

It happened again at Illinois. After an easy win at home against Northwestern, the Hoosiers went to Champaign and got clobbered 89-68. Thomas again was in early foul trouble and wound up playing only 29 minutes, scoring 13 points. There had been some talk early in the week that Woodson might return for the Illinois game, just six weeks after his surgery. Doctors opted to wait another week and it once again showed on the court. When Thomas was good, the Hoosiers had a good chance to win. But whenever he was shackled with foul trouble, the Hoosiers couldn't score enough without him on the floor.

The Hoosiers were 7-5 in the Big Ten and back in the middle of the pack, although no one else was running away with a big lead.

They would all come to regret that.

*** *** ***

**H**elp arrived on Feb. 14 when Woodson returned to face the Iowa Hawkeyes in Iowa City. He had been practicing lightly for a week and looked good when he was out there. When he got the green light, he was ready to go. Everyone was glad to have him back on the floor. They had all seen what he had been going through. The pain of rehab had been immense … and intense.

"Woody came back, but we brought him back too early. Knight probably should have never let him play, but Woody was such a team guy that he wanted to do anything he could to help us," Risley said. "He made such a gallant effort to play, but it was so obvious he was in an enormous amount of pain. It may have looked like he was 100 percent, but he was nowhere close."

It took everything Woodson had just to play in a game. He was hurting so bad that he couldn't practice most days. There were

250

times where he'd play a game, stay in bed for two days sacked in pain, and would play another game and be the best player on the court.

"We all did whatever we could to help him. No one minded that he couldn't practice," Risley said. "We never let him drive. I'd go pick him up. We'd bring him food, run errands for him, lots of us or his girlfriend, who later became his wife. He'd play in a game, but then he couldn't even move for two days.

"I think Coach Knight felt bad too. He's a human being and he saw how much Woody was hurting. But he also saw that Woody wanted to play, wanted to do whatever he could to help us. That's just the kind of guy Woody was. I've known him since I was 13 years old, and he's just the best guy. Not only did he want to win so badly, but he always wanted to do anything he could to help us too."

He came back with a vengeance. And his teammates fed off his return.

The Iowa game was tough. The Hawkeyes were very good – they would reach the Final Four later that year – and always tough to beat at home. Woodson played 39 minutes in what Knight called "one of the guttiest performances you're ever going to see" that night, scoring 18 points. Thomas added 14 points – and 30 stitches – in an impressive 66-55 win.

Thomas got the stitches diving for a loose ball and cracking heads with an Iowa opponent. Seeing it up close from 10 feet away was scary.

Woodson reminisced about it years later in an interview when talking about Thomas' toughness as a teammate.

"My first game back, it's a close game and right before the half, there's a loose ball, Isiah's racing for the ball, another kid's racing for the ball and they collide heads," Woodson said. "It's like

251

a gunshot went off. I get over to Isiah, he's on his knees, he looks up at me — I could see down in his head. His head just exploded. He goes in at halftime, he gets 30 stitches. Today, that's a concussion, you don't play. He came back, played with 30 stitches and we win the game.

"That's one tough kid."

Thomas always said the same thing about Woodson. In a story that's been shared often, Thomas harkened back to that night in Iowa City four years earlier on the night he was named MVP of the NBA All-Star game. Asked the if winning MVP had been

IU Archives P-0055982
Isiah Thomas proved he was a tough kid throughout his freshman year. He even played a game at Iowa after getting 30 stitches in the head.

his biggest thrill in basketball, he replied, "My biggest thrill was watching Mike Woodson come back from back surgery and hit his first three shots at Iowa."

Yes, that's how much Woodson's return meant to his pals.

Woodson followed up that debut with 24 points in 39 minutes against Minnesota in a 67-54 win in Bloomington. He was named Big Ten Player of the Week. The Hoosiers, who had been unranked prior to Woodson's return, suddenly reappeared at No. 13. They even got one first-place vote in the coaches' poll, from Michigan's Johnny Orr.

Call it the Woodson respect factor.

IU won at Michigan State five days later. Woodson played all 40 minutes, scoring 20 points in the 75-72 victory. Thomas also played 40 minutes, which was just as amazing considering he needed more stitches to close a cut over his eye after he was assaulted by a student in his dorm room. He fell after being hit and struck his head on a table on the way down.

They concluded the road trip with an impressive 65-61 win against Michigan in Ann Arbor. Woodson once again played 40 minutes, scoring 24 points. Steve Risley had a huge game in 15 minutes of playing time, including a big outlet pass right on the money to Woodson late to seal the win. They came home and beat Wisconsin (Woodson 16 points in 39 minutes), setting up a winner-take-all scenario for the Big Ten title on the last day of the season in Bloomington against Ohio State.

Indiana won 76-73 in overtime against the No. 9 Buckeyes to win the Big Ten title outright. Woodson played every minute, gutting it out until the end. It was an amazing six-game run for Woodson and the Hoosiers, who passed five teams in the Big Ten race to win the title outright in a year no one thought that was possible.

"They beat Ohio State the last day of the season in what amounted to a playoff game. I think it may have been the greatest game I ever saw at Assembly Hall," said Bloomington Herald-Times sports editor Bob Hammel, who's seen just about every game played in the 40-plus years that Assembly Hall has been around. "When you look back at the lineups and I think seven of the starters that day went on to play in the NBA. And that didn't include Wittman. But both teams just had terrific players, and it was a game for the ages, with IU winning in overtime.'

A few weeks later Mike Woodson was named the Big Ten MVP in a landslide. He had only played six of 18 games, something no MVP had ever done. Think about it, he played a third of his team's games and was still MVP in a league that was loaded with great teams and great talent.

"When Mike came back, we knew that things were looking successful again," IU center Ray Tolbert said recently.

IU would finish the regular season ranked No. 7 in the final poll. They were unranked three weeks earlier. Woodson was back … and those dreams of a national title were back, too.

It was time for the NCAA tournament to start and the Hoosiers once again were back in the conversation when it came time to talking about title contenders. They saw the brackets and smiled. The path to the Final Four was going to very interesting.

Four months earlier, that's all they would have ever asked for.

# Chapter 16

**B**ack in 1980, the NCAA tournament had 48 teams, which meant the top four seeds in each regional got a first-round bye. Indiana was placed in the Mideast Regional as the No. 2 seed and was sent to Bowling Green, Ky., for the first week. Kentucky was the No. 1 seed, and went to Bowling Green as well.

The Hoosiers, with their star Mike Woodson back and playing well, went into that first week of the tournament brimming with confidence, with just one very small concern.

"The way those last three weeks went well with Woody back, we felt like we could beat anybody," IU forward Steve Risley said recently. "To win six tough games in a row like we did to come back and win the Big Ten, that really had us ready. We were ready to make a run. Those championship aspirations we had at the beginning of the season, they were back. Sure they went away for a while in the middle of that season, but they were definitely back. Woody had been that sensational."

The concern? Back then, the NCAA didn't have any restrictions about teams playing on their home court in the tournament. The first-round game that set Indiana's opponent was No. 7-seed Virginia Tech against No. 10-seed Western Kentucky. Even though Western Kentucky was the lower seed, the Hilltoppers were playing on their home court in Bowling Green. A win would give them the Hoosiers … on their home court.

Crazy things can happen in those scenarios. IU didn't really want that to be an option. They were somewhat relieved when Virginia Tech won, taking Western Kentucky out of the picture by erasing an 18-point deficit in the second half.

The Hokies fell behind quickly to Indiana as well, trailing 26-12 midway through the first half. They battled to catch up, but the Hoosiers hung on, winning 68-59. IU made its free throws down the stretch (10-for-12) to stave off a rally. Isiah Thomas led the way with 17 points. Butch Carter had 16, Ray Tolbert 14 and Woodson 13.

Kentucky won too, sending both of them to opposite brackets of the regional semifinals in Lexington, Ky,.

**IU Archives P-0021674**

Steve Risley was an Indianapolis native who provided a lot of toughness for the Hoosiers. His focus on rebounding and defense played a big part in Indiana's success during his career.

Rupp Arena in Lexington … Kentucky's home court.

But the crazy scenarios did play out at the other Mideast Regional site in West Lafayette, Ind. Purdue was just the No. 6-seed in the region, but the Boilermakers got to play their first two NCAA games on their home court. After dispatching No. 11-seed LaSalle in the first round at Mackey Arena, Purdue upset No. 3-seed St. John's, which had a very good team that year. The St. John's people did a ton of bitching afterward about having to play Purdue on its home court. (The NCAA stopped the process a few years later).

Purdue got what it wanted, surviving and advancing the first week with a huge prize at the end, a rematch with Indiana in the regional semifinals in Lexington. It would be their sixth meeting in 14 months, a stretch of showdowns unmatched in the long history of the rivalry.

"We had great battles with Indiana, and that was really rare, playing three times in a year. It was very rare to do it two years in a row," former Purdue coach Lee Rose said recently. "It was a big thing for us going into the next season that our previous year had ended with that loss to Indiana at the NIT in 1979.

"It left a bad taste in the kids' mouth, all of them. There was a certain amount of carryover from that. And it even still carried over into the postseason, definitely. When we were getting ready to play Indiana in the tournament, what happened the previous year came up often. We didn't want them ending our season again."

And the last thing Indiana wanted, of course, was for Purdue to end its season either. It was going to happen to somebody. Indiana looked at it this way: They were a weekend away from advancing to the Final Four and all that stood in the way were their two biggest rivals, Purdue and Kentucky. Winning a regional to get to a Final Four was always sweet, but this was going to be over-the-top sweet, a three scoops of ice cream, covered in sprinkles, covered in hot fudge kind of sweet.

Purdue and Kentucky, in Lexington no less. How great was that?

Oh, and Duke was there too. Had to have a fourth, you know.

\*\*\*     \*\*\*     \*\*\*

The atmosphere around Lexington was incredibly intense, like no regional ever seen since. Rupp Arena held 23,000 fans and change but there were easily more than 100,000 basketball fans in town all weekend. Big Blue Nation was out in force, of course. The Wildcats were back, having won the 1978 NCAA title and convinced – as they always are – that this 1980 title was soon to be theirs as well.

The red-clad IU faithful were out in full force too, invading Lexington in waves. Thousands of people came without tickets to the game, just to be there and, more importantly, to say they were there to all their friends back home.

It was all that important.

"That was one of the most incredible settings for a regional tournament that I had been around," longtime Louisville sportswriter Billy Reed said recently. "Indiana and Kentucky were both very good and everyone expected them to meet in the finals.  I mean, they were the top two seeds. The UK fans were out in force, of course, because the games were in Lexington, but the IU fans showed up by the thousands too.

"There were people everywhere, and everybody wanted tickets. There were some high dollars being paid for tickets that week."

Everyone was looking forward to the weekend's IU-Kentucky showdown of No. 1 vs. No. 2. There was no doubt the IU fan base was, and so were the players.

"We wanted another shot at Kentucky because of the way they had beaten us earlier in the year," Risley said. "Woody was really hurting then (he had surgery a week later) and Wittman went out for good in that game, too. With Woody back, we felt we were better than they were.

"But I'll also tell you this. We would never look past Purdue. Never. Our total focus was on that game. We knew the challenge we had with them."

***    ***    ***

**As you would expect** with such a huge gathering of natural rivals, a lot of this was personal, too.

It certainly was for Lee Rose, the Purdue coach. Lexington was home to him, born and raised. He had first made a name for himself as an anonymous head coach at North Carolina-Charlotte, taking them to the Final Four in 1977 as a relative unknown.

Now here he was with his Purdue team just a few years later, back in his hometown again. (UNCC also advanced to the Final Four by winning a regional in Lexington).

"I was from Kentucky, I went to school right there at Transylvania in Lexington, and UK," Rose said. "My dad died young, but my mother was there and it was really nice for me, because she couldn't get to many games. That was big. It was a great experience."

It meant a lot to Reed, too. Anything IU-Kentucky was big, but having the Lee Rose angle was nice for him, too. Local boy

**IU Archives P-0055996**

Mike Woodson's return from major back surgery in 1980 was one of the most inspirational stories in IU history. He played the last six games of the Big Ten season, all wins, and won league MVP in that short time frame.

made good was a nice story, and they were friends as well.

"For me, the story that weekend was Lee Rose because we had been friends for a long time. Lee grew up in Lexington and we both went to Transylvania College. He's a really good man and I was rooting for him, quietly of course," Reed said. "Lee came from a very, very poor background and grew up maybe a driver and a wedge from Rupp Arena. He worked so hard for everything he's accomplished in his life.

"He had a good team that year, but I think everyone still expected Indiana to win that game. They had been playing really well coming into the tournament. For Lee, this was a dream opportunity, to beat Indiana and Kentucky in Lexington and get to a Final Four. That was special."

And that's why they play the games.

\*\*\*    \*\*\*    \*\*\*

**W**hen you've played a team five times in 14 months, it's not easy to surprise them with anything. Lee Rose knew that. So did Bob Knight. Sure, there would be tweaks here and there but this IU-Purdue matchup in the regional semifinals was going to be all about execution.

"Playing Indiana so often, it's not like there were a lot of adjustments you can make," Rose said. We knew them so well, just like they knew us. You might throw a little defensive wrinkle in there, maybe drop a defender off on somebody now and then, but that's about it. It's all about executing after that. You're not going to fool Knight with anything, and he wasn't going to fool me either. You had to bring your A-game, and we brought it for sure. We stuck to our game plan all the way through.

"We had a game plan that we had a lot of confidence in. We just wanted to keep throwing it in to (center Joe Barry Carroll) every time and force Indiana into some tough decisions, some tough double teams. He played great and also did a great job of passing out to his teammates. We got a lot of good looks in that game and we shot really well early. Joe was outstanding. Everyone played well."

The Boilermakers kept control of the game through most of the first half – "Purdue played with a lot of intensity, which we lacked," IU coach Bob Knight said at the time – pushing its lead to 11 points at the half. "We just came out flat and lethargic," IU's Ray Tolbert said recently.

On the way into the locker room, Knight was giving referee Blaine Sylvester an earful, questioning a call. Sylvester listened patiently, hearing Knight out, which isn't always easy for an official. But the other referee, Lou Moser, rushed over and immediately gave Knight a technical.

Knight was livid. "I'm the first guy to admit that I know when I deserve a technical, but this was missed completely," he said after the game. "The situation was poorly handled."

His blood boiling, Knight exploded when he walked into the IU locker room.

"After that technical, he comes into the locker and throws a Gatorade bottle against the wall and it just explodes," Risley said. "It wound up getting all over him. He had this light blue shirt on, but it was soaking wet and it got all dark. He coached the whole second half with Gatorade dripping off of him."

Purdue came out and made both free throws on the technical, and then scored on their first possession. Suddenly the Boilermaker's 11-point lead had grown to 15.

Knight said the tech had no bearing on the game. Everyone

else disagreed. The Knight technical was a huge turning point in the game.

"No question it was. I thought that issue at the half was really big," Rose said. "When we came back out, we hit the shots and then scored right away to go up 15. From there, we quickly got it to 19-20, we were playing so well. They made a run at the end, but we had a big enough cushion to handle it. I thought that issue at the half was really big."

It's difficult to chase down a good team from behind. Eight or nine points is one thing, but 15 is tough. And 20 is even tougher.

"Once we fell behind, we just couldn't get it all back," Risley said. "When you fall behind against top-level teams, it's really hard to catch up.

"By the time we got to the Purdue game, Woody was completely wiped out. He was running on empty, and it was a very physical game. He didn't have any miracles left. With Woody hurt, we just didn't have enough firepower to get back in it."

Freshman sensation Isiah Thomas tried. He led a late furious rally to try to get the Hoosiers back into it. He finished with a season-high 30 points, but the Hoosiers came up short. Their season – and Woodson's career – ended with a 76-69 loss. Woodson finished with just 14 points and no one else scored more than six.

"Isiah just took over and did all he could. We all did. But they were really good," Risley said.

Rose has enormous respect for Thomas and his performance that night. But he also reminded us that he got 40 points from his perimeter guys, Drake Morris and Keith Edmonson, who had 20 each.

"Isiah scored a lot, and he was just terrific, but our guards scored a lot as well," Rose said. "We neutralized them, I thought, in the backcourt and they didn't have an answer for Joe. He scored

It was in the North Carolina game in December when Isiah Thomas (11) had to take over the IU team. Mike Woodson had gone out with an injury and the freshman point guard was forced into a leadership role.

early and he did a great job of finding open guys when Indiana put extra pressure on him.

"We were scoring pretty well and they just couldn't keep up."

To a man, every IU teammate appreciated all Woodson had sacrificed for them. He had given it his all.

"Unfortunately, Mike just ran out of gas coming back so soon from all of the rehab and pounding his body took through that period of the Big Ten push," IU center Ray Tolbert said recently. "He just did not have that same energy to lead us like he normally would have."

The six games in 14 months between these two arch-rivals were so even. Both teams won three times. Both teams knocked out the other in a postseason tournament. Indiana scored 353 points, Purdue 351. "You can't get any more even than that," Rose said.

But in the only NCAA tournament game the two schools have played, it's Purdue that gets to claim the upper hand. They're 1-0.

"Rose and Purdue beat Indiana in a great game. He had his kids really well prepared and everything they tried against Indiana worked," Billy Reed said. "That was a coach's dream come true that night, beating your biggest rival in the tournament, in the city you grew up in. He was really proud of that game."

All the Kentucky fans in the building loved watching Purdue beat Indiana. They cheered for the Boilers as hard as they cheered for their own team. But their arrogance and crassness disappeared quickly a few hours later when a very pedestrian Duke team upset the Wildcats on their home floor.

The Indiana-Kentucky showdown everyone expected never happened. Both of them lost.

"That was such a strange night, with both Indiana and Kentucky losing," Reed said. "You could just see all the air get sucked out of that building. It was such a terrific setting for a regional, but no one expected it to turn out that way, with Purdue and Duke knocking off the big boys.

Purdue beat Duke two days later in a half-empty Rupp Arena to advance to the Final Four. It was one of the most special moments of Rose's career, winning a regional in Lexington, especially at the expense of Indiana fans. The Boilermakers would lose to UCLA in the national semifinals and Rose would leave Purdue a few weeks later to take a job at the University of South Florida in Tampa.

His time was short in West Lafayette, but he made his

Mike Woodson (center) and Steve Risley hug after IU clinched the 1980 Big Ten title with a win over Ohio State. That's Landon Turner to the right.

mark. Purdue fans will always have that, the 1-0 record against Indiana in the NCAA tournament. "Winning that day in Lexington, it was really special beating Indiana," Rose said.

We'll give them that. We have all of our NCAA championships, of course, and they have none.

Purdue, in case anyone needs reminding, has not been back to the Final Four since then.

*** *** ***

**W**oodson finished his career at Indiana with 2,061 points. At the time, despite missing those 15 games, he finished second on the all-time IU scoring list behind only Don Schlundt (2,192). Based on his scoring average, those 15 games probably cost Woodson at least 300 points. Had he stayed healthy, he would have certainly passed Schlundt and the Big Ten record-holder at the time, Purdue's Rick Mount (2,333).

Woodson was that good.

"As a college player, I think he was the best player in the country," IU teammate Ted Kitchel said. "He wasn't the most well-known player, but I think he was the best. I watched the Pan American Games tryouts, watched practice, and he was such a dominant player and a great scorer and slasher.

"But the most important thing about Woody is he's one of the finest people that you would ever want to know. He's just a great, great individual."

And it's a shame he didn't leave Indiana with a ring. If anyone should have, it was him. He gave IU all he had, playing through enormous pain and fatigue during his senior year. IU went on to win a national title the next year, but Woodson could only watch from afar. Happy for his friends –very happy – but without a title himself. It's one of the great injustices in IU basketball history.

"That was the worst part of it all, Woody not getting a ring. He deserved it so much. I always felt guilty that I got one and he didn't," said Risley, who had grown up in Indianapolis and had known him since he was 13 years old. "I don't think any of us would have minded if Coach had given Woody a ring the next year. For every one of us, he meant that much to us as a player, as a person and as a teammate.

"He's really one of the greatest guys I've ever known."

That's a great way to be remembered. Thousands of Hoosiers fans feel the same way.

"When you look at that 1980 team and the fact they had the Pan Am experience with Woodson and Tolbert and Thomas and I really believe Woodson was on his way to becoming the national player of the year. He was off to a great start," longtime Bloomington Herald-Times sports editor Bob Hammel said recently. "That had a chance to be one of the great Indiana teams ever. Woodson

IU Archives P-20407

Members of the 1980 Indiana basketball team provided some special memories, especially down the stretch in the Big Ten season.

was such a premier player and Thomas was emerging in the back-court and Tolbert was developing, too, at a very quick rate. You look at their scores before the injuries and they were just killing people.

"Woodson was back (but by the NCAA tournament) he's just worn out. He had just stretched himself way too thin."

But that effort to try – and play so well – will never be for-gotten. It's why Mike Woodson is one of Indiana's all-time favorite players.

"I always thought he might be able to come back but I really wasn't sure if he would be any good and be able to contribute because he had missed so much time," longtime radio voice Don Fischer said. "That's tough when you have to spend so much time rehabbing* an injury and just trying to get back. You also lose your conditioning.

"I just wasn't convinced how effective he would be or how much of an impact he would be able to make. That turned out to be a mistake on my part."

It would have been a mistake for anyone to ever question Woodson's heart and his desire to help him teammates win. That's what made Woodson so special.

"To me, that's the greatest testament to the kind of person Mike Woodson is," Risley said. "Six weeks after major back sur-gery, and he's back out there on the court helping us win. He gave us every last drop of what he had.

"That I will never forget. What he did those last three or four weeks was incredible. As far as I'm concerned, it's one of the greatest months in Indiana basketball history. He was spectacular. We couldn't finish it, but I'll still never forget it. Mike was just the best."

Kitchel agreed. He played with a lot of great players, but

269

he considered Woodson to be the best. He too hates the fact that Woodson didn't get a ring, especially because that 1980 was so deserving.

"He was probably the best player that I ever played with," Kitchel said. "The best team I ever played on was not the '81 national championship team, but the 1980 team. It's kind of interesting, if you look at Coach Knight's best teams, the 74-75 team was much better than the 75-76 team because they could score so many more points. They were a much more dominant team, yet they didn't win.

"It's the same with us. I thought our '80 team was better than '81, because of how great Mike was."

# Chapter 17

There's no doubt that the seasons of 1975 and 1976 were the greatest two-year run in Indiana basketball history, where the Hoosiers were one broken arm away being undefeated back-to-back national champions. But two decades earlier, IU almost went back-to-back as well.

Should have, most people say, including the IU players who won a national title in 1953 but then fell short in 1954 despite being ranked No. 1 most of the year.

In 1953, led by All-Americans Don Schlundt and Bobby "Slick" Leonard, Indiana won its second national title in history when it beat Kansas 69-68 in Kansas City. Indiana was dominant that season, winning 22 of its final 23 games and claiming the Big Ten title outright with a 17-1 record.

It was the second national championship for legendary coach Branch McCracken and – shockingly – just his first Big Ten title. He had seven second-place finishes, including finishing second to Purdue in 1940 when the Hoosiers would go on to capture their first national title. IU got the NCAA bid when Purdue opted to play in the NIT Tournament instead.

As good as that '53 team was, many will tell you the '54 team was better. Indiana returned all five starters from the national championship squad and three other players off the bench who had been consistent contributors. Even though we did not include this team in our group of five for this book, it wasn't without months of debate. You can't talk about near-misses in IU basketball history without honoring the '54 group.

271

Indiana University basketball historian Bill Murphy, the author of the book "Branch" about coach Branch McCracken, said on paper the '54 team was more talented than the one that had captured the national title the year before.

"I don't think there's any question about that," Murphy said. "They had so many good pieces and parts to that team and they really had great team chemistry, too. And they had the experience of playing on the biggest stage the year before and winning it all. There is absolutely no question in my mind that IU should have hung a banner in 1954, too."

Center Jim Schooley was the only senior on 1953 championship team. And while the 6-foot-5 star from Auburn, Ind., wasn't around for 1954, he knew what they were capable of accomplishing.

"There's no reason the 1954 team shouldn't have won the national championship as well," Schooley said in an interview in the summer of 2014. "They just ran into a really good Notre Dame team in the regionals and they didn't play their best game. But I really believe if they had beat Notre Dame in the tournament, they would have easily moved on and won the national title for a second year in a row."

Looking back, more than 60 years later, Bobby 'Slick' Leonard still shakes his head when he thinks about what that '54 team could have been.

"In 1953 we had a great ballclub," Leonard said in a 2014 interview. "But we really should have won the championship in back-to-back years. We got upset in the regional in 1954. We should have won. We were ranked No. 1 the whole year and we won the Big Ten championship for a second year in a row. But that one always sticks with me because we knew were good enough to win it back-to-back."

Bob Hammel, the longtime sports editor of the Bloomington Herald-Telephone which later became the Herald-Times, was a
college freshman at IU in 1954 and remembers that team well. But
he had an intriguing theory of his own regarding not only a 1954
repeat but also one with the 1975 and 1976 teams potentially winning it in back-to-back years.

Hammel believes it is so much more difficult to win a title
in back-to-back years than it is to win it the first time.

"I've always wondered to myself how good that 1976
Indiana team would have been if IU had won it in 1975," Hammel
said. "Because I think once you've won it the first time, it does
take an edge off of you."

Hammel said it's difficult to compare the two examples because the structure of the NCAA Tournament was so much different in the mid-1950s and it wasn't as difficult as it would become
later to simply get to the Final Four.

"I always thought that maybe 1953 had a little more going
for it," Hammel said. "They were hungry because it was their first
time really competing for the national championship and I think
that hunger is a big factor."

Hammel said he remembered a headline in a basketball
preview magazine heading into the 1954 season that really gave
him pause at the time. Hammel said the headline read "Anytime
Indiana loses it will be an upset."

"I had never thought of it in those terms, but that's what
that team had to play under," Hammel said. "The pressure was
great every time that team took the floor because of what it had
accomplished the year before. I've heard the theories that the '54
team was better than '53, but I've never been so sure. I'm not
certain that '54 had the same electricity that '53 had because again,
it was all new to them and they were playing in those kind of big

games for the first time."

Schlundt was a junior and Leonard a senior on that '54 team. But the team had other stars, too.

Dick Farley was a senior forward from Winslow, Ind. who had had a solid career for the Hoosiers. Farley was IU's third-leading scorer (behind Schlundt and Leonard) for three years in a row. But Farley was so much more than a consistent scorer. He was an

**IU Archives P-0028885**

Indiana had won a national championship in 1953 and had most of their top players back in 1954, poised to win another title. The Hoosiers were upset by Notre Dame, despite Don Schlundt's best efforts.

excellent defender who always guarded the opposing teams' best player. He was a good shooter, too. As a junior, he led the Big Ten in field goal percentage.

Hammel had nothing but high praise for Farley. He said he has been lobbying for some time to get Farley inducted into the Indiana Athletics Hall of Fame.

"He was that good," Hammel said. "He was always the guy they put on the best opposing player, including the centers, and Dick was about 6-5. He was a terrific player. And then as a rookie in the NBA he was a key player for Syracuse when it won a championship."

Murphy said that Farley and Leonard were the two players that really made the '54 team go.

"Schlundt was the rock in the middle but Farley was a farm-brand player, to use a term from back in those days," Murphy said. "He was a hustler, he was a go-getter, he did the dirty jobs on defense, he could score, he could rebound, he was a player that could really do it all."

Murphy said there was something that stood out to him about Farley – and every member of that '54 team, for that matter.

"Every guy on that team knew their role in every particular game," Murphy said. "It was kind of like some of (Bob) Knight's teams in that roles might change with a particular opponent ever so slightly. They all had a role but those roles might change a little bit depending on who was playing and such. But Farley in particular would adapt his role to fit whatever game or opponent he was playing and that's why I thought he was a special player.

"He would just do whatever it took to find a way to win any particular ball game."

Burke Scott was a junior guard from Tell City, Ind. and started in the backcourt with Leonard. Scott averaged 7.2 points

275

per game on that '54 team.

"Burke would really lock down on the other teams' player that was bringing the ball up the court and he would take it away from him," Schooley said. "That's the kind of player that Burke Scott was."

The late Charlie Kraak was the fifth starter in '54. He averaged 6.7 points per game and "was a tremendous rebounder," Murphy said. "Back then McCracken was known to say that Charlie was the best rebounder on the team."

Wally Choice was a sophomore guard who may have only averaged 5.5 points per game but had some big games later that year in Big Ten play. In a late season game at Ohio State, for example, Choice scored 20 points for the Hoosiers. As a sophomore, Choice was really the only newcomer that was a consistent contributor. Everyone else had returned from the year before.

"Choice was a good player but the bench was not the strength on the '54 team," Hammel said. "They got so much production out of that starting lineup and those guys really led the way."

The stars, though, were Schlundt and Leonard. The combination of "Mr. Outside" in Leonard and "Mr. Inside" in Schlundt was a potent one-two scoring punch for the Hoosiers. Leonard was a shooter who would hit the big shot when you needed it. McCracken had given him the "ice in the veins" label the year before when Leonard hit a free throw in the closing seconds that gave IU the deciding point in the 69-68 national championship win over Kansas.

Leonard played forward as a sophomore in '52, but in both '53 and '54 he played point guard, his more natural position. In 1954, Schlundt and Leonard combined to average nearly 40 points per game which was about 50 percent of IU's offensive production.

Schlundt, who was nearly unstoppable inside and could hit hook shots equally well with both hands, averaged 24.3 points per game. Leonard, whose outside shooting opened things up for Schlundt inside, averaged 15.4 points himself.

Leonard said it was more than just a team of two All-Americans that had the school poised for back-to-back national champions.

"It was just a great ballclub," Leonard said. "Not just the starting five. We had everything covered. All our guys could play, and most of them (15 of 20) were Hoosiers."

Yes, they could play. And they would have a heck of a season, right up to the end.

*** *** ***

Indiana opened the 1954 season as the No. 1 team in the nation. The defending national champions would win the first six games of that season before dropping a 67-51 decision at Oregon State.

It was an interesting scheduling quirk that had IU facing Oregon State in Corvallis, Ore. on back-to-back nights. Apparently, OSU figured if Indiana was coming all the way to the Pacific Northwest for a nonconference game just a few days before Christmas, that the least they could do would be to play two games.

IU, behind 34 points from Schlundt, beat the No. 11 Beavers the first night, 76-72. The second game, Oregon State triple-teamed Schlundt and it was an effective strategy. Oregon State denied Schlundt the ball and IU's other shooters had an off night. The 51 points scored by the Hoosiers were 10 points fewer than they would score in any other game all season.

Following the Oregon State trip, Indiana would open Big

Ten play by winning its first eight conference games.

The third game in the Big Ten that year was particularly significant. Indiana went on the road and beat Minnesota, 70-63. The Golden Gophers had been a tough out on the road for Indiana for some time. Minnesota had won five games in a row against Indiana at home, including a 65-63 victory late in IU's '53 national championship season. That would turn out to be IU's only loss in its final 24 games of the season in '53.

"That was a big, big win for the '54 team," Hammel said. "Minnesota was kind of Branch's nemesis in those days, especially on the road. To be able to go out and beat them in Minneapolis early in that season had to set the tone for what that team was able to accomplish."

IU would rattle off six more wins after that – there was also a non-conference victory over Louisville in that run – to improve to 8-0 in Big Ten play.

In a four-game span, however, beginning Feb. 13, 1954, IU would drop two out of the next four games. One was a 100-90 road loss at Northwestern but then the Hoosiers dropped a lopsided 18-point game at home to Iowa, 82-64. Indiana still had a one-game lead in the Big Ten standings over those same Hawkeyes but the Hoosiers had two conference games left. The first was at Ohio State and the second at home against Illinois to close out the regular season. Illinois was another team that was just one game back in the Big Ten standings.

And to play in the NCAA tournament, you had to win the conference. There were no at-large bids.

The Northwestern game was a tough one because IU had beaten the Wildcats six times in a row and actually that would be one of only two losses to Northwestern in a 14-game span from 1949-59. The Iowa loss was at least explainable because the Hawkeyes would finish second in the Big Ten that year.

Still in '53 and '54, IU was nearly perfect at home. In fact, that loss to Iowa was Indiana's only home loss in that two-year span and to lose by 18 points was significant.

"Indiana had a tremendous home-court advantage back then and if they ever lost, people would really turn their heads," Murphy said.

In the Indiana University Basketball Encyclopedia, written by Jason Hiner, McCracken was quoted at the time as saying his team looked fatigued. Indiana clearly had a bullseye on its back as the defending national champions and it just made things that much more difficult for the Hoosiers. It's the same thing that other Indiana teams would experience in the 1970's, 80's and 90's in particular.

"This team is tired," McCracken said. "Not as much physically as mentally. Every team we've met has pointed for us and gone all out against us. The constant strain of meeting that challenge every night and getting ourselves up for it is showing its effects."

Indiana had an easy time the next game in an 84-68 win over Ohio State in Columbus. Schlundt had another big game with 27 points. The first time the two teams met that year in Blooming-ton, a game won by IU 94-72, Schlundt exploded for 47 points. At the time that was an Indiana individual school record for scoring. Schlundt matched it the following season as a senior, again against Ohio State and again with the game being played in Bloomington.

Only three other players in IU history have ever scored more than 47 points in a game. Sharp-shooting Jimmy Rayl, the 1959 Indiana Mr. Basketball from Kokomo, holds the Indiana school record with 56 points. He did it twice, first against Minne-sota in 1962 and later against Michigan State in 1963.

The second game performance by Schlundt against Ohio State in 1954 may have been 20 points less than his school record but it was still big because it helped IU to a crucial road victory. The significance of that win was that the Hoosiers controlled their own destiny going into the final Big Ten game against Illinois at home.

If Indiana won that game, it would win the Big Ten title outright for the second year in a row. If it lost to Illinois, however, the Hoosiers would finish tied with the Illini and the way the rules worked back then only one Big Ten team could advance to the NCAA Tournament. Since IU had won it all the year before, the conference likely would have given Illinois the next shot to represent the conference in a tie situation.

In the only meeting between Indiana and Illinois that season, Indiana held on to a one-point lead in the closing seconds when Leonard was fouled and got two shots. He made them both and IU hung on for a 67-64 victory that advanced the Hoosiers back to the NCAA Tournament where they would have a chance to defend their national title.

They wouldn't be around for long.

***     ***     ***


**I**ndiana got a bye in the first round and then played Notre Dame in the second round of the 24-team NCAA tournament. The Irish and Hoosiers had been big rivals in recent seasons. The year before, Notre Dame had edged Indiana in a nonconference game and then IU had knocked Notre Dame out of the tournament. This season, the two teams had met in Bloomington back on Dec. 14 and IU had come away with a 66-55 victory.

The NCAA tournament game would be much closer. In

fact, Notre Dame – a first-round winner over Loyola (Louisiana) – deployed the same strategy that Oregon State had used against IU and basically tried to force someone other than Schlundt to beat them.

Notre Dame led by three in the closing seconds, when Leonard drove the basket and tried to draw a foul. He made the shot but was called for an offensive foul. Back then, the basket counted but the opposing player was awarded two foul shots. He made them both. Leonard came down and scored again on another driving layup but this one came as time expired and Indiana had dropped a 65-64 decision to the Irish.

More than 60 years have passed since that play in that game on March 12, 1954, but Leonard is still convinced that there's no way it was a charge. In a 2014 documentary titled *"Bobby Slick Leonard, Heart of a Hoosier"* produced by former Indianapolis Star assistant sports editor Ted Green, Leonard described what he remembered of that play.

"I go in for a layup and here comes a guy in from the left side and they called a charging foul on me," Leonard said in the documentary. "I made the basket but they called a charging foul."

As the story is retold in the documentary it was pointed out again that Leonard still disputes the call to this day. In fact, at one point he sent a photograph to the man he allegedly fouled, former Notre Dame athletic director Dick Rosenthal.

"The picture clearly shows that he didn't get there in time," Leonard said in the documentary. "So that's the only solace I have, that the referee blew the game."

Rosenthal has a different recollection of the play.

"I was standing absolutely still and Bob ran right over the top of me," Rosenthal said.

"He flopped," added Leonard.

"I flopped all right, but I flopped because his knees were in my chest," Rosenthal said with a smile.

Away from the playful banter between the two friends, Rosenthal had another memory of that game, too. It involved a class act displayed by Leonard after that game.

"I'll never forget though, that as disappointed as I'm sure (Indiana) was, Bob Leonard was waiting for us at our locker room door when we left the court," Rosenthal said. "And he congratulated us and wished us well in the tournament. He was a terrific sportsman and a terrific competitor. Bob would beat you any way he could, but when it was all over he was a total gentleman."

Indiana finished that season 20-4, which marked the second 20-win season in a row at IU and just the third in school history. In the next 19 seasons, IU would only surpass the 20-win plateau twice.

"When I think back at my own list of teams in Indiana basketball history that I believe could have hung another national championship banner, that 1954 team would be way up there," Hammel said. "In that time and in that era, they just had so much talent. I still believe though, that they weren't as hungry as the 1953 team and that was ultimately the difference. But when you're just looking at talent, when you look back at that starting lineup that had Schlundt, Leonard, Farley, Scott and Kraak, that was one of the best lineups from top to bottom that Indiana has ever put out on the floor."

Hammel said the 1975 team will always be tops on his own list of teams that just came up short. He said the 1993 team would be second. "But 1954 deserves a mention in there somewhere," Hammel said. "They were simply that good."

Consider it done, Bob.

# Chapter 18

There were several other great IU teams we had to consider for this project, and it's a great thing for IU fans when you consider that there is a mention of every decade of IU basketball since the 1940s in this book.

We've been able to care about great IU basketball for nearly 80 years now since playing for national championships – and hanging NCAA banners – became a possibility.

We are one lucky fan base. We've had great teams that have won, and some great teams that came oh so close. Mostly, we've had fantastic players, many of whom were just as great off the court as they were on it. We've had a couple of legendary coaches too, and that's made it lots of fun – and very interesting.

Here's three more teams we can't forget, plus the bond all of these title chases created among IU players from year to year, and generation to generation.

And here's just a little more about the only player who was a big part of this "Missing Banners" project who can still do something about it.

\*\*\*      \*\*\*      \*\*\*

Branch McCracken had some great teams in his 24 years as the Indiana University head basketball coach. He won national titles in 1940 and 1953, had a No.1-ranked team in 1954 and finished either first or second in the Big Ten in 12 of those seasons.

But the team McCracken would often brag about the most

was the 1960 Indiana Hoosiers.

"(Former IU coach) Lou Watson told me one time he thought that was Branch's best team," said Bob Hammel, the long-time sports editor of the Bloomington Herald-Times. "He said that Branch had told him that he thought that was his best team, too."

The 1960 team, led by powerful center Walt Bellamy, went 8-1 in nonconference games but had a couple of hiccups early in conference play, which would be devastating in an era where only the conference champion advanced to the NCAA tournament. IU would win its final 12 Big Ten games of the conference season, but it wouldn't be enough.

The Hoosiers finished second in the Big Ten behind an Ohio State team that would go on to win the national champion-ship. The Buckeyes were led by Hall of Famers Jerry Lucas and John Havlicek, a got a little help from a bench player named Bob Knight.

How good were the Hoosiers in 1960? Consider this: As part of its season-closing 12-game winning streak to end the con-ference season, Indiana clobbered No. 1-ranked Ohio State 99-83 on Feb. 29, 1960, the second-to-last day of the Big Ten season. It would be the only game OSU would lose all year. They won the national title four weeks later, beating its four opponents by an average of 19.5 points per game.

But they didn't beat Indiana. Indiana would finish the season ranked No. 7 in the nation – and wasn't allowed to play in the NCAAs.

"I've always believed that had things been set up then the way they are now, with multiple teams from a conference going to the NCAA Tournament, that Indiana could very easily have won the national championship that season," said Bill Murphy, IU historian and author of the book "Branch," about the life and times of Branch McCracken. "Indiana was playing its best basketball at the end of the year and it beat the eventual national champions by 16 points at home on the second-to-last game of the year. If that team had played in the NCAA Tournament, I have little doubt that it would have won it all."

What set the '60 team apart from most of the teams in that era was its size. Bellamy was a 6-foot-11 junior center from New Bern, N.C. He was joined in the frontcourt by 6-7 senior Frank Radovich from Hammond, Ind. and 6-6 sophomore Charley Hall from Terre Haute. In that day and age, that was a monster front line and the Hoosiers were able to dominate most opponents inside. Both Bellamy and Radovich averaged double-doubles. Bellamy led IU with a 22.4 per game scoring average and 13.5 rebounds. Radovich was at 14.8 points and 11.9 rebounds. Hall chipped in 5.8 points and 5.3 rebounds.

Add it up and the three-player IU front line checked in with more than 42 points and 30 rebounds per game. "That was an imposing front line for that time," Murphy said. Senior guard Bob Wilkinson and junior guard Herbie Lee gave McCracken a potent starting five.

And it was another team of homegrown Hoosiers. Twelve of the 15 players on the roster were from the state of Indiana.

Indiana's only nonconference loss was to Missouri. There were several early big wins, including one at Butler against legendary coach Tony Hinkle, which always meant a lot to McCracken.

But then the Big Ten season started, and it started poorly.

Indiana was upset in its home opener by Purdue, losing 79-76. Then the Hoosiers went on the road and lost at Northwestern, scoring only 57 points against a team that was just 3-9 at the time.

"Indiana averaged 83 points per game that season but sometimes teams have an off night shooting and that's what happened to Indiana at Northwestern," Murphy said. "They just couldn't hit a shot."

Now IU was 0-2 and faced unbeaten and top-ranked Ohio State in Columbus. The Buckeyes were 11-0 overall and 2-0 in conference. Indiana played them well and actually led 95-90 in the final two minutes before Ohio State scored the game's final six points and posted a 96-95 victory.

"Indiana just outplayed them the entire game and deserved to win," Hammel said. "But at the end of the game, IU missed a couple of free throws and turned it over a couple of times and ended up getting beat."

Suddenly, the Hoosiers were 0-3 in conference play and had pretty much eliminated themselves from the Big Ten title and ultimately postseason play in just a matter of weeks.

Indiana would go on to win the final 12 games of the season and the most impressive victory in that 12-game run was the Feb. 29, 1960 win at home over Ohio State when the Hoosiers pounded the Buckeyes 99-83. It should be noted that the Buckeyes had already clinched the Big Ten title, but Ohio State was still fighting to keep its unbeaten season alive.

Hammel said that Bob Knight was always quick to point out that his team had already won the Big Ten title before it lost to Indiana that year.

"And I would tell Bob, 'Oh yeah and I'm sure whenever your teams would clinch a title you'd just let them go out and do whatever they wanted to from that point on?' " Hammel said. "That would get a smile out of him anyway."

Even though Indiana knew it was out of the conference race, the Hoosiers still felt as if they had something to prove in that game. They felt, and arguably so, they had given the game away in Columbus earlier in the season.

In the second meeting, Bellamy scored 24 points and all five IU starters scored in double figures. That game was memorable in Indiana circles for another reason, too. It was the final game played in the Old Fieldhouse that had housed IU basketball from 1928-1960. The 8,000-seat arena was home to IU's first two national championship teams (1940 and 1953) and was also the arena that Indiana played in when Branch McCracken was an All-American.

In fact, McCracken scored the first points ever in the fieldhouse in 1928.

*** *** ***

**In Bob Knight's second year** on the IU campus, magic struck early. Way before anyone expected national champion runs out of Knight and the Hoosiers, the 1973 team came together quickly with a talented roster of young and old and made a stunning run to the Final Four.

Knight, the fiery boy genius, was only 32 years old.

The Hoosiers were led by All-American center Steve Downing and fellow senior John Ritter. Downing averaged 20.1 points per game and Ritter was second on the team at 14.7. They were veterans who had been through the Big Ten wars and both were exceptional in the tournament run. They were also the only players on the roster with any college experience.

It was the kids who made this all work. The rest of the contributors on that team were newcomers. Steve Green and John Laskowski were sophomores who each averaged 10 points a game. It was their first season of varsity action because freshman couldn't play a year earlier.

Thankfully that rule changed and freshman Quinn Buck-

287

ner, Jim Crews and Tom Abernethy all played quality minutes on this '73 team. So did sophomore John Kamstra. Those six, along with Downing and Ritter, were the only ones who averaged more than 10 minutes a game.

Knight inherited Downing and Ritter when he arrived at IU, and he was fine with that. They became two of his favorites. But the rest of the roster needed to be filled, and the youngsters stepped right in and contributed. IU would win the Big Ten by sweeping its final four games and finished the regular season with a 19-5 record.

It was an accomplishment that came much earlier than expected.

"The rule change that allowed freshman to play was huge

IU Archives P-0055997
Steve Risley and Mike Woodson are all smiles after the Hoosiers won the Big Ten title on the final day of the season against Ohio State.

288

because then Quinn Buckner and Jimmy Crews could play right away with us," Laskowski said. "Because Steve (Green) and the rest of us had to sit out the previous year, it was nice that we all sort of came on the scene at the same time.

"Scott (May) and Bobby (Wilkerson) where there too, but had to sit out that year because of the academic rules back then. But the rest of us were ready to contribute right away, and with Downing and Ritter we suddenly had a pretty good team."

Back then, Knight was among the hardline group of coaches that preferred freshman waited a year to play. In that first season of the rule change, people weren't sure how Knight would handle it. He was happy to have the sophomores like Green and Laskowski ready to go, but the freshman he wasn't so sure.

Quinn Buckner changed all of that.

"I think Quinn singlehandedly changed Coach's idea about playing freshmen," Laskowski said in a 2015 interview. "Quinn started right away and he was just a great natural leader. He led our team in assists that year and Jimmy Crews was second. They stepped right in."

Winning the Big Ten was a pleasant surprise, as was beating No. 5 Marquette and No. 17 Kentucky in the regionals at Nashville, Tenn. That wasn't supposed to happen … but it did.

"The progress we made as a team was incredible. I mean, we're just freshmen sophomores in 1973 we reach the Final Four when no one expected us to and here we are playing UCLA, a team that wins every tournament and just dominates back in those days.

"A few years later, that's us, with everyone looking up to Indiana. With Indiana dominating just like UCLA did."

Indiana lost to Bill Walton and UCLA in the national semifinals. The Bruins won 70-59 and would finish the season as undefeated national champions. The game was much closer than the final score. The battle between Downing and Walton was epic.

"Making that kind of tournament run that early in our careers was really important down the road," Laskowski said. "By the time 1975 rolled around, we had all played together for a long time. We had built a great bond. That rule change really helped our '75 team because we were all basically in it together right from the beginning."

That 1973 team couldn't be considered as a banner favorite because the awesomeness of UCLA and the historic run they were on – 88 straight wins, eight national titles in 10 years – but what the Hoosiers did that season was impressive nonetheless.

And it set the stage for greatness going forward. That core group of youngsters became part of the great 63-1 run in 1975 and 1976 that included a national title and unbeaten season in '76.

\*\*\*     \*\*\*     \*\*\*

The five championship games that Indiana have won have to be the start and finish of fans' favorite NCAA tournament games for the Hoosier Nation, but next on that list is probably a bit of a generational thing. The 2002 win over No. 1 Duke was sweet, but for many the biggest other win came in 1984, when a slightly above average Indiana team beat No. 1-ranked North Carolina in the regional semifinals in Atlanta.

That was Dean Smith's best team ever. Michael Jordan, Sam Perkins, Brad Daugherty, Kenny Smith and Matt Doherty were the stars, but an Indiana team that entered the tournament with a less than impressive 20-8 record beat them.

It was a total shock. The Hoosiers, after all, had staggered into the tournament, losing three of their last six Big Ten games.

They beat Richmond 75-67 in the first round in Charlotte, but they were less than impressive.

North Carolina was next in Atlanta and no one expected anything from the Hoosiers. Basketball pundits were already salivating over a dream Final Four with Jordan and the Tar Heels, Akeem Olajuwon and the Houston Cougars and Patrick Ewing and the Georgetown Hoyas.

No one was talking Final Four or national championships about Indiana. And with good reason. The Hoosiers had been off the national radar all season. They were ranked No. 19 in the Associated Press preseason poll, but fell out immediately after losing their season opener to Miami of Ohio at home in Assembly Hall.

They wouldn't return to the rankings until mid-February, checking in at No. 17 for a week after a seven-game winning in the Big Ten season. But they lost at Northwestern the next game and were never heard from again in the polls.

They entered the NCAAs not really sure what to expect. They got a No. 4 seed, which many pundits thought was far too high. They were led by freshman guard Steve Alford, who started his brilliant IU career impressively by averaging 15.5 point per game that season. He shot 58 percent from the field and 91 percent from the free throw line that year.

Uwe Blab played well at center and averaged 11 points per game. No one else averaged in double figures. No one.

Indiana's win over North Carolina in the 1981 championship game was still fresh in the minds of the collection Hoosier Nation fan base, but this was different. Jordan's legendary status will come later, but in 1984 he was already considered the best college player in the country, and there was no doubt. He hit the game-winning shot as a freshman to win a national title for UNC in 1982 and he was a stud his sophomore and junior years. Everyone knew he was turning pro and the experts all figured he wasn't going to leave without a national title. UNC was 28-2 and its two losses were by a combined three points.

Come game time, Dan Dakich got the call to guard Jordan, who was national player of the year and about to become an NBA superstar. Dakich only started nine games all year and averaged a pedestrian 3.9 points per game, but he could guard.

And, for some reason, the Hoosiers actually thought they could win. They were basically alone in those thoughts.

"We actually were pretty confident going into that game with UNC. Indiana had a history of beating them in the NCAAs and every day of practice with Coach Knight was all about preparing to win," Dakich said during an interview in 2015. "He treated North Carolina no different from any other team we would play. We had a plan."

Dakich, who now hosts a radio show in Indianapolis and also works for ESPN, gave a great description of Knight's plan during an interview with ESPN.com's Grantland website a few years ago.

"We had a meeting at six o'clock on Sunday after we beat Richmond and Coach Knight came right in, and he closed the door to the locker room," Dakich told ESPN. "He said, 'All right, we're going to whup North Carolina's ass. And anybody that doesn't 100 percent believe we're going to whup North Carolina's ass, you need to get the f--- out of here right now.'

"And he said, 'Here's exactly how we're going to do it. This is how you handle Jordan, this is what we're going to do." And I remember walking out of there thinking, '*Damn, we're going to be ready. Whether we can do it or not, I don't know, but we're going to be ready.' That's for damn sure.*"

292

*Knight didn't give out defensive assignments until a meet-ing three hours before the game. He gave out the first four assign-ments and then, as Dakich recalls, gave a disgusted glance Da-kich's way and said "You've got Michael Jordan."*

The Detroit Pistons made the "The Jordan Rules" for guarding the legend famous a few years later, but for Dakich his rules came right out of practice and the notes that he kept. Take away the back cut. Take away the offensive rebounding. Don't let him post you up.

And that was it. Simple, basic defensive principles that Knight preached all the time anyway. "We just wanted him to shoot jump shots," Dakich said. "All we tried to do was take away the things he liked to do most."

There are plans on paper, but then there plans on the court. This time, they translated. Every IU player bought into the fact that UNC may be more athletic and more slick, but they definitely weren't tougher. They challenged them physically, and the Tar Heels didn't really respond. Dakich recalls the IU players laughing when UNC guys were raising their fists for Smith to take them out of the game. "We weren't coming out for nothing," Dakich said. "We were going to fight them right to the end."

Jordan scored two quick baskets on Dakich in the first minute – "and I'm doing the math in my head, thinking he's going to score 160," Dakich can say now with a smile. But from there, he battled him. And when Jordan picked up a second foul, Smith took him out for the remaining 12 minutes of the first half."

The North Carolina fans had two takes on that. They've always argued the second foul on Jordan was bogus. They also ar-gued that Smith had more to do with stopping Jordan than Dakich did, sitting him for all that time. So be it, Dakich says.

"I busted my ass that game, boxing out to keep him off

IU Archives P-0029285

Dan Dakich became something of a legend the night Indiana upset No. 1 North Carolina and Michael Jordan in the regional semifinals in 1984. He was credited with shutting down Jordan, the greatest player ever.

the boards and defending him the paint as hard as I could. I just went at him with all I had," Dakich said. Jordan would finish with only 13 points on 6 of 14 shooting and IU won 72-68. Dakich only scored four points and had three assists, but his defense on Jordan became the stuff of legend.

Steve Alford was the star for Indiana. He scored 27 points and put on a show. Even with a roster full of future NBA stars, it was Steve Alford who was the best player on the floor that night.

"Alford was fabulous," Dakich said in 2015. "That's what I always loved about Steve; he wanted the big moments. Even as a freshman, he showed up and worked and you knew he was going to be great. He wasn't just this shooter from Indiana, he knew how to win.

"Things got a little hairy late in that game. We started missing some free throws and Steve just demanded the ball. He's ducking in and out of people, drawing fouls. He didn't miss (making 9 of 10 free throws) and we won. It was pretty awesome."

The euphoria didn't last long. Less than 48 hours later, Indiana faced an unheralded Virginia team in the regional finals and lost 50-48. They went from the highest of highs to the lowest of lows in a matter of hours, losing to a Cavaliers team that already had 10 losses on the season and was eminently beatable. Point guard Othell Wilson was the star of that team, and former Indiana Pacers coach Rick Carlisle also was a starter.

Virginia's goal was to keep the ball out of Alford's hands, and that's exactly what they did. Alford managed to make just two field goals in seven shots and scored only six points on the day. Virginia's defense was stifling.

"We figured we win against North Carolina and then who knows? Final Four, baby," Dakich said. "But then I blew the next game with Virginia. I turned it over with 1:18 left and I'll never forget it. That one was on me. We were horrible that day."

Pace of play had something to do with it, but the 48 points were the fewest Indiana had scored all year. Still, it was a memorable weekend in Atlanta.

"We had our moment there, that's for sure. But that would have been a tough title to win," Dakich said. "We would have had to beat Olajuwon and Ewing at the Final Four."

That would have been a tall order, even for the man, the myth, the legend Dan Dakich. He still at least gets to milk the I-shut-down-Michael-Jordan stuff all these years, and he does it in fun, in his own self-deprecating way. It's all good.

"Michael just ran into a better athlete that day," he says with a smile.

*** *** ***

**T**here is an undeniably strong bond between IU basketball players through the generations. Certainly in the 29-year run by Bob Knight, all of his former players share unbreakable common bonds. There's been some disconnects since then, and that's a shame, but hopefully time heals all wounds.

Part of doing a project like this is that we're mostly reminiscing about bad things, about teams and players that came up short. We ache for players like Steve Green and John Laskowski, great seniors who missed out on a national championship in 1975. It hurt for all the players on that team, but many of them won the following year. It was the same with the 1980 seniors, especially Mike Woodson. He missed out, but many of his teammates won the following year.

Still, there is always a sense of being a part of these levels

296

of greatness. Laskowski, for instance, felt like he shared the great run in '76 with his former teammates, even from afar as he travelled all winter in the NBA.

"In '76, I paid very close attention to what they were doing," Laskowski said in a 2015 interview. "I'd watch them whenever I could. I remember the Michigan game when (Kent) Benson had the tip-in at the buzzer to win it, I'm on the road and I'm yelling and screaming with my arms up when we won. People thought I was crazy.

"And that championship game, I watched it alone in my apartment on my little TV and I loved every minute of it. I'll be honest, I started crying when they won, I was so happy for them. They accomplished their goal, winning that title and going undefeated. It's awesome that 40 years later, no one's done it again. After my NBA season ended, I went to Bloomington on Little 500 weekend and saw them all. It was great to celebrate with them and see how excited they all were. I felt so good for them. I mean, those are my guys."

It was the same with Woodson. For many of the players on the 1981 championship team, they carried a little bit of their friend with them to a title the following year. Beyond being a great player, Woodson was a great leader and a great friend. As great as Isiah Thomas was in 1981, it was because he got to play with Woodson the year before.

"I think it was really good for Isiah to spend a year with Woody," former IU teammate Steve Risley said. "Woody was a quiet guy, but when he spoke you listened, and you believed what he said. He was a great leader, just not in a rah-rah way. There's no doubt Isiah had a little bit of Woody in his heart in '81 when we won.

"The worst part of all that was Woody not getting a ring.

He deserved it so much. I always felt guilty that I got one and he didn't. I don't think any of would have minded if Coach had given Woody a ring the next year."

Those early Knight teams had greatness written all over them, and not just on the court on game days. They were hard workers, and they were classy people on and off the court. They were what Indiana basketball was all about, and every player had to hear about it for 30 years.

"It was funny through all those years later," Laskowski said. "So many IU players would say to me 'We didn't like you guys at all. Every time we'd make a mistake or Coach didn't think we were working hard enough, he always go on and on telling us that 'the '75 guys would never allow that.' I guess we set the bar

IU Archives P-0055945
That docile-looking young man in the sweater is Bob Knight. As a young coach, he built a dynasty with his 1975 and 1976 teams going a combined 63-1. Knight is pictured in 1975 with Quinn Buckner (left) and Scott May.

pretty high."

And being attached at the hip through the years does mean something. It will mean something again in January of 2016 when the 1976 team is going to be honored at Assembly Hall on the 40<sup>th</sup> anniversary of its undefeated national championship season.

The 1975 guys have been invited to be honored at the same time. Much as Hoosier Nation considers those two seasons to be all one group, so does IU athletic director Fred Glass. Both groups are going to be feted.

"The athletic department called me to let me know they were going to honor the 1976 team this year, but that they wanted all the guys from '75 there as well," Laskowski said. "They want to honor the greatness of that two-year span and I have to tell you, it's so nice that they want to include us in that celebration. It really means a lot to me."

It means a lot to all of us.

***     ***     ***

**Throughout all the pages** of this book, we've chronicled more than a hundred IU basketball players who gave their heart and soul to Indiana University and did all they could to get another banner to hang in Assembly Hall. And they all have a soft spot in the hearts of Hoosier Nation for all that effort.

But of all those players, there's only one who can still do something about it.

Yogi Ferrell.

The exciting point guard decided to come back to IU for his senior season in 2015-16 because he "wanted to leave a legacy."

Another year at the helm of what should be a very good IU

**IU Athletics**

Of all the players interviewed for this book, the only one who can still do something about hanging a banner is Yogi Ferrell, who's back for 2016.

basketball team will catapult Ferrell high up in the record books in many categories. It also gives him one last chance to hang a banner.

Ferrell said he has often found himself daydreaming as he stared at the five national championship banners in the south end of Assembly Hall.

In his dream, he can picture what that sixth banner would look like.

"Believe it or not, I actually have done that. I do think about what another banner would look like up there. No question about it," Ferrell said.

"In my mind I just move those five over a little bit and hang another one up there just to see how it would look and I think it would look pretty nice."

That's what we all think.

# *About The Authors*

## *Tom Brew*

Tom Brew has been an award-winning sports writer and newspaper editor for more than three decades. He is an Indiana University graduate who was born and raised in Schererville, Indiana. He has worked at the St. Petersburg (Tampa Bay) Times, the Tampa Tribune, Indianapolis Star and South Florida Sun-Sentinel and has covered Indiana basketball and national college basketball as a writer and editor for many years.

This is Tom's second book. His first book, a novel called **The Ties That Bind**, was released in 2014 to critical acclaim and deals with the perils of gambling addiction among college athletes and best friends. Tom also published a collection of stories in 2012 called **A Season Inside: Lake Central Basketball**, which covered the final high school season of current NBA player Glenn Robinson III and his Lake Central High School teammates in St. John, Indiana.

Tom has three grown children and two granddaughters. He still writes and edits on college sports and also owns a book publishing company.

To purchase other books or to inquire about other future projects, contact Tom by e-mail at **tombrewsports@gmail.com**

## Terry Hutchens

Terry Hutchens knows Indiana University basketball. He is beginning his 18th season covering the Hoosiers, the first 15 at the Indianapolis Star. He currently is the content manager for Btownbanners, a free fan site at www.btownbanners.com and does freelance work for the Associated Press out of Indianapolis. This is his seventh book and sixth on IU sports topics. Five times, Terry has been honored as Indiana's Sportswriter of the Year by the National Sportscasters and Sportswriters Association. He also teaches sports journalism at Indiana University in Bloomington. Terry and his wife Susan have been married 29 years and live in Indianapolis. They have two grown sons, Bryan and Kevin.

Terry's other six books: A new book in 2015 is titled *So You Think You Know Indiana University Basketball (We'll see about that),* which is an IU basketball trivia book that has separate chapters with trivia on players, coaches, national champions, venues, Bob Knight as well as much more. *Hoosiers Through and Through*, published in 2014, took a look at the best IU basketball players of all time who hailed from the state of Indiana. *Rising from the Ashes,* published in 2012, looked back at the resurgence of IU basketball brought along by Cody Zeller, Victor Oladipo, Christian Watford, Jordan Hulls and company. In 2007, his book *Hep Remembered* looked back at IU football coach Terry Hoeppner, who died from the effects of brain cancer while still the IU coach. Two years later, he wrote a book with Coach Hep's widow, Jane Hoeppner, that was a Christian/inspirational book titled '*Never Ever Quit.*' His first book, in 1995, was about the Indianapolis Colts called '*Let 'er Rip*. In 2013, he also wrote the updated second edition of the *Indiana University Basketball Encyclopedia*, originally written in 2004 by Jason Hiner.

# *Thank yous*

A project like his can't be done with just two writers. There were many other people involved that deserve a mention of thanks.

First off, to all the dozens of Indiana University players and coaches who took the time to reminisce with us, thank you very much. There are a lot of never-before-told stories in this book, and your candor and honesty is very much appreciated. And thanks as well to the opposing coaches and players who brought great insight to many of these seasons through the eyes of the victors and fellow competitors.

Special thanks go out to Bradley Cook, the Curator of Photographs at the Office of University Archives & Records Management at Indiana University in Bloomington. His time and patience in finding photos through the years for us is greatly appreciated. And thanks to Mike Dickbernd of IU Athletics for his photos from the 2013 season.

Terry and I both want to take the time to thanks our families and friends for being patient with us through this project, which was fast and furious at times. Special thanks to Phil Mahoney and Jennifer Wright for lending a hand when I really needed it, and thanks for the patience of librarians across Indiana and Florida who provided a nice, quiet place to write.

Two other groups also deserve a mention. Thank you to everyone involved with the IU Alumni Association, both in Bloomington and also chapters all around the state and country. They are big supporters of this project and we are happy to donate a portion of the proceeds of this book to scholarship funds for local chapters. We will be setting up book signings and watch parties throughout the country and all those events will be posted on my www.hilltop30.com website. You can also follow us on Facebook and Twitter at **@tombrewsports** and **@IndySportsHutch**

Lastly, thanks to all of you Indiana University basketball fans. You are the best fans in the country and your passion is unquestioned. So, please, keep the faith.

– *Tom Brew*